Praise for Randa Jarrar

Him, Me, Muhammad Ali

Winner of the 2017 American Book Award
Winner of the 2017 PEN Oakland/
Josephine Miles Literary Award
Winner of the 2017 Story Prize Spotlight Award
An *Electric Literature* Best Short Story Collection of 2016

"Sharp and irreverent . . . When Jarrar's sense of humor tangles with her character's feelings of estrangement, the results are often charming and funny."   *—Los Angeles Times*

"Funny and darkly imaginative . . . The stories are confessional and riveting by means of the deeply intimate and vulnerable spaces Jarrar's characters allow us to access . . . Jarrar's fiction has exciting range, and she investigates narrative as well as social taboo . . . Like the tightrope walker in the opening story, Jarrar pulls off incredible feats again and again."   *—Portland Mercury*

"These stories showcase the strength and talent of a writer of immeasurable gift and grace, who confronts the poignant and often brutal realities her characters face with sass and verve."   *—The Los Angeles Review of Books*

"Weird, hilarious, melodramatic, gorgeous, and sincerely resonant."   *—Electric Literature*

"Jarrar presents an astonishing variety, each story as inventive as it is insightful. It's a book for this oppressive electoral season, where presidential politics are ugly and destructive, and demagoguery is endeavoring to trample a core American truth: Our country's strength derives from open borders. Jarrar is here with a correction."   —*The Millions*

"As a queer, Muslim, Palestinian-American and proud fat femme, Jarrar lives the complexities of intersectionality. Fortunately for her readers, she infuses those complexities into her characters . . . She shows their connections and differences by leaving no topic unexplored—class, language, and sexuality are all at the core of the book. Her style is straightforward and direct while being multifaceted and thought-provoking."   —*Bitch*

"Jarrar follows up her novel, *A Map of Home*, with a collection of stories depicting the lives of Arab women, ranging from hypnotic fables to gritty realism . . . Often witty and cutting, these stories transport readers and introduce them to a memorable group of women."   —*Publishers Weekly*

"A subtle interrogation of class spanning multiple generations and an exploration of desire enlivened by a dash of magical realism."   —*Kirkus Reviews*

"[A] brave, bright, tell-it-like-it-is collection . . . Impressively varied in style and content, Jarrar's collection is recommended for a wide range of readers."   —*Library Journal*

"*Him, Me, Muhammad Ali* is a searing collection of short stories about loving, lusting, losing, and surviving. Randa Jarrar is one of the finest writers of her generation. Her voice is assured, fiercely independent, laced with humor and irony—and always, always, honest."

—Laila Lalami, author of *Conditional Citizens*

"Randa Jarrar's prose is bold and luscious and makes the darkly comic seem light. The voices in *Him, Me, Muhammad Ali* are powerful individually and overwhelming as a chorus. This wonderful work isn't just a collection; it's a world."   —Mat Johnson, author of *Loving Day*

"These vibrant, funny, earthy, and above all, yearning (for love, for family, for home) stories are a revelation. Jarrar combines the invention of Calvino, the sprung style of Paley, the poetic imagery of Babel . . . But that mash-up isn't mere stylistic exuberance; it's a restless, relentless and deeply affecting effort to forge identity out of fragments, to make a whole out of halves. These are the stories we need right now."

—Peter Ho Davies, author of *The Fortunes*

"The stories of Randa Jarrar are fearless, funny, and sad, soaring and earthly, fable-like and visceral, full of families, lovers, friends, strangers, and lonely children. These stories laugh with and think through and rise against, which is just to say they brilliantly demonstrate Jarrar's huge talent, compassion, and range. *Him, Me, Muhammed Ali* astonishes from start to finish."   —Sam Lipsyte, author of *Hark*

A Map of Home

"[An] extraordinary debut . . . Jarrar's lack of sentimentality, and her wry sense of humor, make *A Map of Home* a treasure." —*People* (four stars)

"*A Map of Home* will leave you laughing out loud."
—*Entertainment Weekly*

"Randa Jarrar takes all the sappy, beloved cliches about 'where you hang your hat' and blows them to smithereens in her energizing, caustically comic debut novel."
—*The Christian Science Monitor*

"In Randa Jarrar's *A Map of Home*, Nidali, a refugee from Saddam's bombs, finds a Texan adolescence dizzying to navigate with her Egyptian-Grecian-Palestinian background. Jarrar's prose is as delightfully dry and intense as her main character . . . Sarcastic essays, Arabic lyrics juxtaposed with American rap, and other anecdotes present cross-cultural observations that are both humorous and wistful."
—*Oxford American*

"Jarrar . . . has created a tale of crossing borders (geographic, sexual, cultural, and otherwise) that challenges readers to remap the boundaries of 'normal' adolescence." —*Bitch*

"Ah, eccentric families. In Jarrar's first novel, the lovable Ammars are talkative, argumentative, and so alive they practically burst off the page . . . Jarrar is sophisticated and deft, and her impressive debut is especially intriguing considering her clever use of recent Middle East history."

—*Booklist*

"Jarrar is a funny, incisive writer, and she's positively heroic in her refusal to employ easy sentimentality or cheap pathos . . . A coming-of-age story that's both singular and universal—an outstanding debut."   —*Kirkus Reviews*

"Jarrar's sparkling debut about an audacious Muslim girl growing up in Kuwait, Egypt and Texas is intimate, perceptive and very, very funny . . . Her exhilarating voice and flawless timing make this a standout."

—*Publishers Weekly* (starred review)

LOVE IS AN EX-COUNTRY

LOVE
IS AN
EX-COUNTRY

A MEMOIR

RANDA JARRAR

CATAPULT
NEW YORK

This book is a memoir. It reflects the author's recollections of experiences over time. Some names and identifying details have been changed to protect the privacy of individuals.

ISBN: 978-1-948226-58-5

Jacket design by Adalis Martinez
Book design by Wah-Ming Chang
Map illustration by Leila Abdelrazaq

Library of Congress Control Number: 2020942072

Printed in the United States of America
1 3 5 7 9 10 8 6 4 2

For my friends

SEDONA

FLAGSTAFF

SANTA FE

CONNECTICUT

CHICAGO

CHESTNUT

10 LOAVES PITA BREAD
YASMEEN BAKERY

DETROIT

EL PASO

MINNEAPOLIS

MARFA

ST. LOUIS

JESUS IS WATCHING YOU
1-800-4-JESUS
♥ADULT♥ SUPERSTORE EXIT 69

MISSOURI

OKLAHOMA CITY

LOVE IS AN EX-COUNTRY

1

THE LOUDEST
WHISTLE

In the summer of 2016, my son now an adult and a sabbatical ahead of me, I decided to drive across the country alone.

I had read about the Egyptian dancer and actress Tahia Carioca doing a cross-country American trip once in Edward Said's *Reflections on Exile*; he interviewed Carioca and she told him she'd been married at least a dozen times. When he asked her what she thought of America she had said, "Liked the people, hate their government's policies." She was born in Egypt in 1919. I was conceived in Egypt almost sixty years later, and here I was, an American woman who had never crossed her own country by car.

But the deeper I dug into Tahia Carioca's trip, the less I

found about it. She had indeed married more than a dozen times: I found the names of fourteen of her husbands. One of them was an American lieutenant she had met while she was dancing at the Cairo Officers' Club during the Second World War. "I whistled the loudest," he boasted to Associated Press reporters after they married. She was twenty-five or twenty-six, a young woman who had already been dancing for ten years. She loved to dance, she always said, but hated the stereotypes about dancers. Of these, she told an American newspaper in 1946, was the idea that dancers lead a life of exotic leisure. "In the movies," she said, "the dancers drink big goblets of wine, eat at rich banquets, and flirt with everybody. Actually, I . . . lead a rather simple life to keep my weight down and my muscles lithe." I found photos of her fifty years after this interview; in them, she is fuller, big bellied, with fat arms and a gorgeous round face. By then she was finally leading the rich life she had so fully earned.

Carioca's dance style was unique: the *L.A. Times* once called her a "belly-rina," but she despised the term *belly dancer*, and said she was an *Eastern dancer*. She was right; the term *belly dance* is Occidental, and in Arabic this kind of dance is called *raqs sharqi*, or *Eastern dance*. Belly dance, as it is known and practiced in the West, has its roots in, and a long history of, white appropriation of Eastern dance. As early as the 1890s in the U.S., white "sideshow sheikhs" managed dance troupes of white women, who performed belly dance at world's fairs (fun trivia: Mark Twain made a short film of a belly dancer at the 1893 fair).

Carioca honored her practice and tradition's roots in Egypt and believed they were beautiful and sacred, and when she danced, many commented that she moved in sharp yet languid movements and took up very little space, moving and contorting herself while grounded onstage.

•

Her 1946 marriage ceremony made news all over the U.S.: she and Colonel Gilbert Levy wed ten years before the Lovings married, and twenty years before *Loving v. Virginia*, when the Supreme Court struck down the last laws of segregation banning interracial marriage. Carioca was very light-skinned and almost passed for white; in a black-and-white photo of her holding Kim Novak's hand and standing near Ginger Rogers, I delight at the thickness and darkness of her Masry hair, notice how much larger and more unique her facial features are compared to the blondes. She is a North African woman charming Hollywood with her smile and her eyes, two of the things she once said were the true secret weapons of a dancer.

I finally found mention of the road trip in a *New York Daily News* article from June 1, 1946: it said that Carioca and Levy would be traveling to New York by motor after spending a honeymoon in Los Angeles, and that afterward, they would split their time between Cairo and L.A.

Twenty years earlier, in 1926, many of America's "highways," still only gravel roads, were completed—it wouldn't be until the 1950s that proper highways were constructed.

These early iterations offered the scenic route cross-country, meaning that the trip could take two weeks and often longer. When, in 1946, Carioca made the trip with her new white American husband, how much privilege did her skin color, her wealth, and her white husband afford her in the middle states?

•

Inspired by Carioca's boldness, I decided to go on a cross-country trip of my own. Unlike Carioca, I was not famous or wealthy or a professional dancer. But like her, I was fond of dancing, light-skinned and privileged, libidinous, divorced more than once, and ready to motor. In Fresno, California, I made a list of destinations.

But before I left for my trip, I flew to Washington State to say goodbye to my favorite ~~lover~~ fuckboi at the time, M. When I arrived, he gave me the worst news you want to hear from a fuckboi you're trying to fuck on a fuckation for the last time: he was falling for a new woman, and he also ("unrelated," he said) had chlamydia. So I pretended not to be sad and took a ferry to Vashon Island and stayed there, in a cabin, for a week. The cabin had a large claw-foot tub where I could cry, sink, and soak my entire body.

My friend T, who lived in Seattle, came to the island to check up on me. T has written books of poetry and worked in tech and is Egyptian. He was one of my Others. You recognize these people: siblings you have never met. The siblings you would choose if you could choose siblings. Friends without benefits, as T would say. We are both fat and beautiful.

•

T said Seattle's dating scene was oppressive. When I asked how, he said everyone wanted to hike, or ride bikes, or camp, or canoe. He wanted to know why he couldn't just watch a movie with someone and fuck. I told him Netflix-and-chill was a thing. He said it was not a thing in Seattle. T was older than me and the women he met were all "fighting against wrinkles and death." T said it was easier being a Christian in Cairo than it was being a couch potato in Seattle.

T and I terrified everyone at a brunch place on the island. We were the only people of color and he kept saying the word *suicide*. He was talking about his depression, but the woman in fabric sandals and a crocheted tank top seated near us was shifting uncomfortably across from her salad. When we left, we saw two young Black men sitting in chairs outside a storefront and we greeted each other instantly, helping erase the memory of the uptight woman at brunch.

Afterward we walked to a marijuana clinic I'd driven past the day before and were told that we needed a prescription. I got angry and I asked T in Arabic if we should tip the woman or bribe her to give us weed. I was joking but he looked at me seriously and said, Maybe we should. I said no and we walked back to my rental car.

Except we walked past the rental car and past the two young men again. They were sharing a joint back and forth. I noticed and T noticed, too. We had to turn around because we had walked past the car. We passed the young men again. They greeted us again. We got in the car and as soon as I started it, T said, We can't ask those guys for weed.

And I said, Of course we can't.

We can't get those guys in trouble, he said.

I agreed with T. I told him that yes, it's racist to ask the only two Black people we have seen today on the island for weed.

T said we should go to Seattle and score legal weed. This involved taking a ferry, which is beautiful and romantic, even in a friends-without-benefits kind of way, and I agreed, and we drove past the two guys as they continued to pass the joint between each other.

T wanted to know why I planned to drive cross-country. Since it was 2016, I told him that I wanted to commune with the land I lived on, to see America during that deeply troubled and troubling election year.

To look at the place that might elect a person like Trump.

I told him I loved the feeling of forward motion, that driving felt like home. And then I told him about Tahia Carioca.

She did the trip twice! I repeated to T. She didn't even live here. She had a tendency to do things multiple times, I said.

T understood, and said yes, she was married more than a dozen times.

LOVE IS AN EX-COUNTRY • 9

Every time she wanted to fuck someone, she had to marry them, I said. There was no privacy.

T agreed. Then he asked me to watch the road.

There were no squirrels on the island, but there were deer. In the five days I stayed there, I had to avoid three deer crossing the road. A deer crossed now, gorgeous and graceful.

"Tahia?" I yelled after the deer.

"Tahia!" T said, "You are beautiful in this new form."

2

MAGIC

I guess most people newly freed from responsibilities take naps. But not me. What I did was, I drove fourteen hours to Arizona, which I realized was a huge mistake as soon as I arrived in Flagstaff. My dog and I slept in a motel room that inexplicably had four beds of varying sizes. We were Goldilocks. My dog, who has thick cataracts and is blind, sniffed at the walls. The next morning I tried to drive us to Sedona, but I realized halfway there that the terrain and view were replicas of Kings Canyon, which was forty minutes from my house in Fresno. But by then it was too late. I was behind a row of cars whose drivers were elderly, their feet fluttering constantly against their brakes. When we pulled into the resort area, I found a way to turn around and began making my way to New Mexico.

An hour in, I stopped at the gas station; my dog hates the car so I took her with me to the restroom after I pumped gas. We squeezed into the restroom, which was busy with a matriarch and her daughter and her daughter's daughter, all Native women, all instantly kind to me and my dog. The stalls were full except one, and when I got out, the women were gone. Instead, a white woman in a uniform was washing her hands. I stood by her and washed my hands, too.

This place is a shithole, she said.

I think it's rather nice, I said.

The bathrooms across the street are like a four-star hotel, but I can't go there, she said, because I'm a truck driver, and we don't get to decide where we stop.

She was wearing a pair of wraparound metallic blue trucker shades.

Some people just shit in their trucks and throw the bag out the window, she said.

They do? I said, amused.

Yes, well the people they got driving now, they're not from here. They're not American. They're Syrians. Might as well hire monkeys to drive trucks now.

I'm glad they got out of Syria, I said, now that I understood that this woman had waited for all the Brown people to leave the bathroom, and that as soon as she saw me, a light-skinned woman who she assumed was white, she was able to be comfortable and vocal in her racism.

Are ya? she said, vaguely disgusted.

Yes, I said. They've been through hell. I'm Palestinian, I said, and for the first time, I realized I was taller than her.

She walked away and said, Well, I hope you're OK with spending your tax dollars on them.

I am, I said. My tax dollars pay for my son's school, for the roads I drive on, and for bombs that kill Arabs, by the way.

She didn't say anything. I could have left, but I went after her. She had hidden in the convenience store's aisles. When I saw her, I said, I'm not a monkey. You're a racist. You have no idea what it's like to be a refugee.

It has happened before: a person thinks I'm cool with their racism, or, more confusingly, when they find out I'm queer, with their sexism.

I got back to the car and held my dog and shook.

•

Children get their first taste of invisibility before they can even remember. Then, they thrill in magic tricks. A parent can hide and then surprise them with their sudden return. Birthday clowns make coins disappear. Children watch cartoons where a mouse takes a dip in a paint pot that holds invisibility ink. Harry Potter wears a cloak, women in Canada and America and Afghanistan and Lebanon and France wear niqabs, humans are surveilled through closed-circuit video cameras, drones can spy activities from high above and can also strike men dead, or hit a wedding party. Once the wedding party is gone, so are the children. If you kill all the children in one family, you have made invisible all the more Arabs, because now the entire lineage has been erased. Death becomes, as my mother says, a return to that amniotic nothingness.

•

To be Arab in America is to be a mouse unwittingly dunked into a paint pot of invisibility ink. It's not that Arabs don't exist. It's that you prefer that they remain invisible unless you can trot out a good one or an especially bad one. It's against your best interests—I almost wrote "*our* best interests"! You've convinced me that my own erasure is good for me— to allow other Arabs to appear. You say, Arabs are only 1.5 percent of the American population. Why must you hear from them or see them more than 1.5 percent of the time?

•

The first magic trick: we are nothing. In the womb, we are invisible to everyone, even to our mothers. Women report intense dreams for weeks before they give birth. For months we carry them, not knowing what they look like, and within them, worlds are already forming, more worlds that we can't see. Here, I am employing the royal *we*. For what are mothers if not sovereign?

•

A short, incomplete list of ways to make it so that when anyone in America pictures an Arab, that Arab is dead:

Ensure that their governments do nothing to help them. These governments disappear people; they imprison, torture, and kill. There are many ways they kill—I won't bore you. You already know all of them.

Leave gaping vacuums of power in their homelands so that any violent group can plant itself in those vacuums and take over. When this happens, it's wonderful, because this group then kills the locals for you. When they start killing your own, you now have the perfect excuse to go in and kill them and even more Arabs.

If Arabs make their way outside of their native lands, it's imperative that they remain erased. This is done by hoping they'll stay home. Segregation in housing and land works perfectly this way. When Arabs live next to white people, sometimes they get killed. The men who kill them are wolves, but they are not alone. Not at all.

Create a trope of what an Arab is. That image is the only one people can see when they think of an Arab that's alive. Make sure that image is as wildly inaccurate as possible. Make sure it's someone who is *not* an Arab, dressed in a costume you create to signal Arabness. Give them eyebrows. A nose you can hang a coat on. Hair everywhere. Culturally inaccurate gowns and headdresses, plus weapons you built or sold to them hanging from their waists. If they don't use those accessible weapons and instead use what they can source—swords, knives, bombs, airplanes, rocks from the land itself—*they* are the savage ones.

Once the trope is created, it functions as a giant subconscious eraser. (For example: An Arab goes on a date with a white American. The Arab tells the white American, "I'm Arab." The white American says, "Well. You don't *look* like an Arab.")

The next step is to make it so that Arabs themselves begin saying this to each other. The authentic Arab in their minds is the Arab trope you created. Now, Arabs in Detroit, Paris, Toronto, Palestine, London, Lebanon, Egypt, and many other places will say, "Well. You don't *look* like an Arab," when they see an Arab that doesn't fit in with what the Arab trope looks like. There is then an enormous deficit of authentic Arabs. In this way, you get Arabs to erase other Arabs.

See?

No?

Well. That's *the point*.

3

BUSHED

In April of 2018, I found myself launched into the middle of a free-speech war between the racist "alt-right" and what they view as Liberal America. I had traveled to Tunisia to attend the Tunisian Book Fair, which had invited me to present my work. The fair was held in a small convention hall, and though every event, panel, and bookseller was indoors, there was a metal ashtray stand outside almost every bookstall. I had a sore throat and walked through the smoky stalls, picking up books in Arabic. One stall carried rainbow-colored Qurans, delightfully queer in their brightly colored pages. Another boasted large poster maps of Africa. I bought an Egyptian novel and walked up the stone stairs to the second floor, where the panels, talk, and presentations were taking place, and entered a heavily attended room.

The panel was on disabled writers and readers, specifically addressing the needs and concerns of the visually impaired. Two of the speakers onstage identified as blind. One wore her sunglasses and a cane and spoke in a quick Tunisian accent—Arabic, French, dialect—that I didn't understand. This was true of all Tunisians. They understood me, because I speak Arabic in an Egyptian dialect, and so much of television and film comes out of Egypt. So in conversation they would kindly adapt their dialects so that I could understand. Things wouldn't be as easy for me at the book fair, and I was prepared. I took a seat, chewed a cough drop, and tried my best to decipher what was being said.

Soon, a visually impaired man joined the stage and spoke at length. At some point, another blind man stood up and asked a question at the microphone. A few minutes later, not happy with the answer, he stood up, shouted at the man onstage, and huffed out of the hall. At least seven other men did the same, following him. All the men held walking sticks and wore sunglasses.

I got out of my seat and followed the men to see what had happened. When I got outside, they were all smoking cigarettes and shouting, blowing off steam. I asked one of them what happened, and he said that the man onstage was an elitist who silenced them and pretended to speak for all blind writers in Tunisia. Soon, the men were escorted back into the hall by a book fair volunteer, who assured them that they would have a chance to share their opinions.

I was staying in a hotel right on Bourguiba Avenue, where

the Arab Spring had begun seven years earlier. The avenue is not wide by American standards—really, what is?—but it features a pedestrian central lane, where people of all ages strolled, with trees and bushes planted on either side of the street. The night I'd arrived, there was a Palestinian right-of-return festival being held near my hotel, in a tent that had been erected in the central pedestrian lane. For hours, I heard Mohammed Assaf's rendition of the Palestinian resistance song "Raise Your Keffiyeh Up High" blaring up into my window. Tunisians love Palestinians, and it was strange to be in a country that so openly displayed this love.

To be Palestinian is often to be silenced, erased, demonized, vilified, and monstrosized. In America, Palestinians are terrorists, mooslems, ugly, violent, fetishized, traumatized. In much of the Middle East, they are an old problem during a time when there is an ongoing new problem, that of Syrian refugees. In Tunisia, where the PLO was exiled after Israel's war in Lebanon in 1982, Palestinians are celebrated and exalted.

•

My throat got more and more sore after the book fair. I stayed in bed for forty-eight hours, ordering a spicy local soup through room service three times a day.

On the third day, I woke up feeling much better.

I wore a floral dress and placed my camera on a window ledge, set its timer, and jumped on the bed to get a shot of myself in midair. I was facing the street where thousands of marchers had walked, fighting for their freedom. I hadn't jumped on a bed since I was a child, or maybe since my own son was a child. I jumped and jumped and jumped until I broke the bed.

I had broken beds fucking before. Always broken beds with another person there. But now I was breaking beds alone. I could do it now all by myself.

When I got back on the floor and inspected the crushed wooden slats, I saw where my body had freely bounced up. I was no longer ill, and I felt free.

•

The taxi driver who took me to Sidi Bou Said said the streets were filled with police because the president was traveling through the area. This president had won with only 55 percent of the votes. I told him this was unlike Egypt, which had a president who'd claimed 90 percent of the votes. Egyptians are not like us, he said. We are a much smaller country, and much angrier. I agreed with him, and I offered my admiration. Soon, we were by the sea, and the area surrounding us reminded me of Alexandria in the eighties, directly after Sadat's rule and before Mubarak had pilfered and plundered the country to shit.

The small sea village where I had rented a house was cobblestoned pathways and alley cats by the dozens. Every building was painted white, with borders, wooden shutters, doors, and window frames a shade between azure and cobalt blue. Some of the doors were yellow. The mosque at the end of the street where I was staying was under construction, and four men worked at its minaret, smoking cigarettes and shouting to one another. The other end of the street was an alley, and at the end of the alley was a cemetery, a large olive tree, and a drop down to the sea. To the north of this was a lighthouse, which I didn't notice until much later that night, when I was on the rental's rooftop and saw its light flashing brightly in intervals.

•

I walked down to a cliffside café that served tea and hookahs. On the way, women and children gawked. In America, where half the population is fat, there are many regions where such microaggressions occur, but as a smaller fat, or someone whose body still fits in store-bought clothes, most comments I receive in person are positive, remarking on my personal style. Americans are usually polite unless I'm in an airport, where the transitory nature of the setting gives tacit permission for men to openly stare at women's breasts and bodies. In the Middle East and Europe, fatphobia runs on the surface, and there is no polite code around it. The obsession with thinness is heightened with the obsession of policing bodies in general, and women's bodies most particularly.

This obsession is most probably, in my opinion, imported from Europe and North America, where women's

bodies are controlled and influenced by hegemonic capital-
ism. Imagine people all across the western Northern Hemi-
sphere waking up in the morning and believing that they
don't need anything to be beautiful but their own selves. The
ensuing market crash would make our financial systems un-
viable. As a person who identifies as femme, I don't mean to
invalidate some people's need for makeup and clothing that
better helps them identify, celebrate, and move through the
world as women.

In Egypt, obesity is at 62 percent, and yet it is socially
acceptable to greet friends and family and coworkers with
"Hello! Have you gained/lost weight?" A remark on another
person's size is normalized.

A list of other things that are normalized: police brutality,
military rule, dictatorships or ceaseless presidential terms,
corruption, job and housing discrimination, criminaliza-
tion of premarital sex, and the dominance of patriarchal and
white supremacist beauty ideals. It is very difficult to love
oneself and to love one another under such conditions.

In the sea village in Tunisia, women elbowed each other
and glanced at me and laughed. I expected this, as I'd experienced it in France, and also in Lebanon. It is worth noting
that Lebanon and Tunisia have both been colonized and oc-
cupied by the French.

I approached two women in their late sixties who had
laughed at me and asked them what it was about me that was
funny. I did this as an anthropologist, curious more than
angry. They wouldn't respond. I asked again, saying, is it my

clothes, or is it my size, or both? The women's husbands finally said, "Bahia." I asked them what that meant, and they said, "You are beautiful." I hadn't expected that.

Men in Tunisia were kind to me. None harassed me, which was different from Egypt, where street harassment is pervasive and dangerous. In the evening, I went to dinner at a traditional restaurant. In the entrance of the restaurant was a shrine to Nelson Mandela: a framed photo of him in Tunisia, a large bouquet of flowers beneath it, and a plaque commemorating his contributions to humanity written in both Arabic and French.

I sat in the dining area and ordered myself some fish tajine and local wine. The wine logo was a bunch of grapes in the shape of Africa. I didn't want to ever go back to America.

Later that night, I walked back to the house rental, and stray orange and white cats followed me almost all the way up the cobbled streets home. The mosque at the end of the street was quiet. Three men walked a few yards behind me and I felt completely safe.

When I got into bed, I decided to check the news on Twitter before I drifted off to sleep. I saw that the Women's March account, as well as a few other accounts, tweeted that Barbara Bush, George W. Bush's mother, had died. What shocked me about the tweets was their veneration of the matriarch, some hoping she would rest in power. She had lived in power. A few days after this, during her funeral, two Secret Service men would stay by her coffin's side. She was safe, even in death.

I was angry—as every woman of color in America is. The matriarch of a war family had passed at the age of ninety-two, and when, years before, reporters had asked her about her son's impending war in Iraq, and the deaths that would inevitably occur as a consequence to that war, Barbara Bush's response had been as follows: "Why should I waste my beautiful mind on something like that?" In a way, she had spoken ill of the dead before they were even dead by saying they weren't worth a momentary thought. Before this comment, she had dragged Anita Hill, saying that she didn't believe she had been sexually harassed or that Clarence Thomas was a predator. And years after the Iraq comment, she called Black evacuees in Houston, who were seeking refuge from the horrors of Katrina, lucky to be living in better circumstances than what "they're used to." She even went so far as to say that their presence in Texas was frightening. "It's scary," she had said.

Because I was angry at the media's positive, hagiographic representation of her, and that women were tweeting their support of her, even in death, I took to my own account and mimicked the praiseful format I was seeing surrounding her death. I wrote: "Barbara Bush is a smart, generous, and amazing racist who, along with her husband, raised a war criminal. Fuck outta here with your nice words."

To further explain my point, I reiterated my beliefs in a way that mirrored W. Bush's 9/11-era rhetoric: he had said that Americans were either with the government or against it, against terrorists or with them. So I wrote, "You are either with these genocidal pieces of shit or against them. It's really that simple." And the majority of (white) America proved to me that they were with genocide.

America is an amnesiac.

To be a woman in America, a mother, and a descendent of North Africans and West Asians is to be the opposite of an amnesiac. It is to be reminded in your bones, your muscles, and the twisted strands of your DNA, every moment of every day, of war, of fear, of expulsion, of discrimination, and of others' fear, dehumanization, and murder, of you and of people like you.

•

Within minutes, white supremacist tweeters had forwarded my tweet to Ben Shapiro, who then directed his thousands of followers to attack me. And they did. When I thought I was in conversation with other women activists, I became suddenly in conversation with white nationalists and trolls. It was late night in Tunisia, and it seemed like a few minutes later, it was late morning.

I was running on adrenaline and Mandela shrines and local wine and freedom.

When a troll found out that I taught at Fresno State, he said I should be fired. Others echoed this sentiment. I wanted to make sure that people reading my timeline knew that I knew my rights: that tenure would protect me from being fired. Later, I would also remember that my First

Amendment rights were the actual thing that was protecting me from losing my job, since I work at a state institution. Soon, incensed by what I said about being protected by tenure, trolls said I had "bragged" and "taunted" them, and they released my work email and phone number, and then my department chair's number. I intervened. I didn't want my phone to ring off the hook and bother my colleagues in the neighboring rooms. I didn't want my department chair, a kind woman nearing retirement age who is into Hot Topic and pop culture, to be assaulted with calls and trolls. So I tweeted that folks angry with my tweet should contact the university president, whose salary is four times the salary of my chair, and whose office is, I believed at the time, better equipped to deal with calls. The president was a person of color who had encouraged his faculty to Be Bold (that was his slogan). I truly believed that he would protect me.

Soon, I received a surprising email from my dean, whom I admired, policing my tone, and telling me to find more constructive ways to talk about these events, claiming that my private tweets are not really private because I represent my department wherever I go. This was a shock to me since I was on medical leave at the time, resulting from anxiety and panic attacks I'd had on the job. I had expected my dean to protect me, too.

Trolls began saying I would need a lawyer soon, and that I was too fat and poor to be able to afford one. In addition, they said, I was too ugly for anyone to care what I had to say—this while they were actively caring about what I had to say. And they said that I would lose writing opportunities for what I'd said and how I'd said it. Amazed at the level of vitriol directed at me, I tweeted out my salary, which can be easily found online since it is public. By doing this, trolls said, I was "boasting."

More hate mail began to pour into my university inbox. The responses all featured, in one way or another, commentary on my appearance, specifically, of my body.

Here, I offer a sample:

May 1

██████ ██████ < ████████@gmail.com>
to rjarrar
How did you get so fat?

Apr 20

██████ ██████ < ██████████████@gmail.com>
to rjarrar
You're an unhinged vengeful camel CUNT:

http://www.foxnews.com/us/2018/04/20/bush
-hating-fresno-state-professor-passes-out-fake
-number-floods-crisis-hotline-with-calls.html

I hope you get criminally prosecuted to the fullest extent of the Justice system. You belong in a G'tmo cell with the other Islamic terrorists.

Speaking of which, I owe them an apology because I just saw a picture of you. You definitely wouldn't make it as their sex slave. You're so obese and ugly you'd make a freight train take a dirt road!

Have fun in prison, cunt!

May 1

██████ ███████ < ████████████ @yahoo.com>

to rjarrar

Barbara Bush was a woman of Grace and compassion you on the other hand are fat Arab Pig you may not think you're going to get fired but I wouldn't bet that you won't wind up Underground you're a disgrace and should be punished appropriately

April 30

██████ ████ < ██████ @gmail.com>

to rjarrar

Aren't you a rancid fat whale of a cunt! Hope you get AIDS sucking one of those white dicks you speak of. But I can't imagine any white man going anywhere near your smelly fucking fat ass! I can't wait until you fucking die bitch . . . i might make a special trip just to take a shit on your grave! Looks like you one or two Twinkies away from it fatty!

That women writers and thinkers and leaders receive death threats and are critiqued for their appearance rather than their arguments is nothing new. But my son and my sister and my brother also received death threats. Of all the email I received at my work address, I received 880 messages that included a racial epithet and/or a suggestion for me to die. All because Barbara Bush's passing conjured, for me, the pain and suffering that the Bush dynasty has caused, whether it be through oil deals, enactments of laws that lead to the suffering of Black Americans, prison investments, or the bombing of Afghanis and Iraqis and the continuous theft of their resources.

Yet the only First Lady we have, as a culture, been allowed to malign viciously was our only Black First Lady. Regardless of what I think of her and her husband's policies in the Middle East, it was beautiful when American children could actually *see* Black people in a position of supreme power. But the beauty ended there. When trolls said I would never say anything so impolite about Michelle Obama, they were wrong. But anything I say to criticize her won't be racist.

Out of all the emails that I received, a majority forecast my impending death. If I wasn't going to die from a bullet, they argued, I would die because my own body would kill me.

For three years before this incident, I had been writing this book about my body, about the ways in which women are held to impossible standards—their bodies expected to adhere to Eurocentric, thin beauty ideals. Women are supposed to carry and birth children, but they are not supposed to talk about the sex they had to get them there. Queer mothers and people who can carry children and choose their own routes to parenthood are silenced or made invisible. And as I write this, there is fear that *Roe v. Wade* will be overturned. America hates its women. And America wants to own its women.

I actually admit I got fat from eating poorly while being poor, being genetically predisposed to diabetes and retaining adipose tissue, and being so lazy and tired after writing books and raising my child alone that I didn't exercise. In fact, I ate. That shouldn't be in the past tense. I eat.

And I also write what I like. And say what I like. And fuck whomever I like.

•

When I woke up the next day, I learned that someone had released my home address in California and my personal phone number. I believed this was utter madness, so I searched for twenty-four-hour crisis hotlines, for trolls and angry people to call, since I believed that attendants at a crisis hotline were a lot more equipped to receive angry, unhinged phone calls than I was. And I was right. Everyone who called got through. The director of the center said that no one who needed help was blocked from reaching a counselor.

And yet, when trolls discovered that I had shared a crisis hotline rather than my own phone number, they became even more enraged. Until this day, there are people online who find this to be an offense punishable by death. I have literally received death threats over this.

What followed was surreal. Many times, I wondered if I was on acid, or in a strange, lucid dream. Major American newspapers, as well as the UK's *Guardian* and *Daily Mail*, repeated what trolls had written: that I was a racist for calling Barbara Bush a racist; that I had flaunted my tenure and taunted my opponents; and that I was disgusting, embarrassing, and impolite.

I watched, amazed, as TV news anchors repeated this. But the part that amazed me was how often they repeated what I had written: that Barbara Bush was "a smart, generous, and amazing racist who, along with her husband, raised a war criminal. Fuck outta here with your nice words." I'd look at another news piece, and again, the anchor would repeat, "Barbara Bush was a smart, generous, and amazing racist who, along with her husband, raised a war criminal." *Fox & Friends* said, "Barbara Bush was a smart, generous, and amazing racist who, along with her husband, raised a war criminal."

The message I wanted out in the world was out in the world. It may have been heavily framed as disgusting and controversial, but it was out there.

In a way, we had won.

I kept a low profile as soon as I got back to the States, aching for the freedom I'd experienced just two years earlier, a woman and a dog driving cross-country.

4

TRUTH OR CONSEQUENCES, 2016

In 2016, after leaving the awfulness of Arizona, I stayed in New Mexico for a week, in the countryside outside of Santa Fe. One morning, I woke to the news of fifty dead in Florida. Fifty gay people. Murdered.

A few minutes later: that the shooter was Muslim.

A little while after that: he identified with ISIS.

A few hours after that: he was gay and went to the club often.

I visited a plundered Native site, gave respects, prayed, and cried.

•

To take my mind off things, I swiped right on every human on Tinder. Matching with none of the women, I decided to go on a date with H, who had been messaging me nonstop. He took me to the central square to look at the Don Diego de Vargas statue. We stood in front of it and he told me the colonial history of the city. He said that every year, the town does a reenactment of the violence and of the parade the Spaniards put on after recapturing the city and murdering Natives in 1692. He told me that although he was part Pueblo, he once took part in that reenactment parade by playing de Vargas himself, on a horse, in costume. He didn't seem too ashamed, which I noticed. I asked him if he ever thought about the twelve years that the Pueblo resisted the Spaniards in the region. He didn't say anything, and he walked me to a spot he said Pueblos congregated in to plan their resistance. The sun was setting red and blue and the place where we stood felt like fire.

H was a handsome, assured-looking man, and he was insecure and eager. I was excited.

He told stories about his parents. My mother was a revolutionary, he said, my father just liked to get laid. He told the stories exquisitely, slowly. He was so good that I never felt trapped when he started a new one right as he was finishing the one before it. We acted chic about our divorcé-ness. His wife had left him for a man who owned a tanning-salon empire. I had heard so many stories like this from male friends. I told

H that I knew a man whose wife left him for her yoga instructor. How could someone make a choice so clichéd? Money, he said. After that I got to experience being Shahrayar, a spoiled king, while he Shahrazaded me around Santa Fe. He showed me the irrigation ditches around the land-grant homes, told me he was Spanish, argued with me about whether he was white—he wasn't—and when I asked him what it was that made him want to marry his last wife, he stopped, then said, I just wanted someone to love me. Then he told me that he was about to say the whitest white-guy thing ever uttered, so I prepared myself. He said, She was the kind of woman Bono would have called up to the stage with him. Wow, I said.

He drove fast, to a hill overlooking all of Santa Fe. We walked around and found a bench and sat there together, our hands on each other until we came.

•

A day later, I drove away, south, away from Northern New Mexico to Truth or Consequences. Every few miles a sign would announce that I was leaving a reservation.

Now leaving Santo Domingo Reservation.

Now leaving San Felipe Reservation.

Now leaving Isleta Reservation.

Reservations all named after Spanish conquerors, genocidal.

•

The drive was less than four hours long. I arrived in Truth or Consequences in the hazy afternoon, the sun beating down and blanching the sidewalks, sending heat off the asphalt. I checked into my motel and the attendant told me that the room I was staying in had been floated, along with the rest of the row house, down from Elephant Butte Lake in the early twentieth century. After she left I washed my hands in the sink, and the walk from sink to bed was wobbly, as if the wood plank floors were still over water. I curled up with my dog on the bed and slept for a long time.

When I came to, I read a list of the dead—they were calling it the Pulse nightclub shooting.

All three days I was in Truth or Consequences, I soaked in a mineral hot tub. I cried and floated and felt an intense loneliness—not solitude at all, just plain painful. And from there, I drove to Texas, crossed the border, parked my car at the El Paso airport, and flew to Minneapolis. There, I attended an Arab American literary conference I had spent the past year helping organize. I lived all week with Arab Americans and Muslims, so many of us queer, dancing, talking about art. I'm so proud of us. I need us. I love us. I wish we could spend our whole lives in celebration, communion, checking on each other, loving each other, being free.

•

The day after the conference, I had a night argeeleh at the Sphynx Café in Minneapolis with the Palestinian poet S and her friend, a Lakota poet. We sat on the sidewalk and the sky was purple and the rain came down and didn't drench us. I pretended to be a m'allemah, a neighborhood bosslady thug, legendary in Egypt, and I spat a monologue loudly. An Egyptian man, just breaking his fast and smoking a cigarette, rounded the corner and came to our table, looking terrified. I told him I was pretending. A few minutes later, he came back, this time right up to where we sat, and I asked him if he was scared of me. I knew he was. He said, Never. I never get scared. S and I laughed and laughed.

•

I flew back to El Paso from Minneapolis. From El Paso, I drove to Marfa. I was surprised to see that Texas had its own border patrol agents, and at the checkpoint, they asked me if I was a U.S. citizen. I said yes. They let me through. In my bra, a half-smoked joint. My happy fat Arab heart.

5

WEST TEXAS, 2016

In Marfa, one of the women writers staying at the Lannan Foundation flipped over on her bicycle and had someone drive her to my house. He knocked on the door and shouted, "Your friend is in the car and needs your help." I came out to find her biting down on a bloody towel. "My fucking teeth got knocked out," she said, and I helped her get in my car and gave her a pack of ice.

We drove to the nearest dental-emergency place, a trailer thirty miles east. We passed a giant border patrol blimp and I tried to distract my friend, who had done terrifying journalism work and was now obviously too vulnerable and battered by the actual fucking soil of Texas.

In the trailer, my friend allowed me, someone she didn't know very well, to care for her. I took deep breaths and promised myself after each one that I wanted to get better at letting others love me.

•

A week later, I kept that promise to myself, and I invited my friends E and A, old neighbors from Austin, to come visit me. I delighted at the sight of them in my driveway, the two of them gorgeous and smiling. Together we drove to the Marfa thrift store, where we saw three confederate flags in a vase. I asked the cashier, an ex–New Yorker, why they had them. He said they were donated and that we could have them for free because he knew we would destroy them. We put them in the trunk, then took them to a field and destroyed them. We wanted to set them on fire but the desert was dry.

•

In the morning, we drove fifty-four miles through the high desert out to Balmorhea State Park, home to the world's biggest spring-fed natural pool. There, we each received citations for drinking beer by the water. Other people were drinking out of koozies, or hiding their liquor in the cooler. We were drinking openly and Officer Teel did not like that. I argued with him for half an hour, but he just gave me an additional note on my citation for "language." He categorized me as white. I told him I was not white. He asked what I was.

I told him. He put me down as white anyway. The pool was full of small fish and catfish. We left as soon as Officer Teel was gone.

At night, we made shadow puppets in front of the Catholic church in town and I rang the church bell and thanked the nun for her service to Jesus. I pissed on a fire hydrant. We disturbed a man named Bill, a visual artist, and he let us into his studio. We climbed up to the roof and climbed back down. Thank you, Mother! I screamed at the sky, the black void.

This is where *Giant* was filmed, everyone here will tell you. I had never seen the film, but I came to learn that it was James Dean's last role before his untimely death. The film featured Mexican and Mexican American actors and was made in 1955. A group of local actors who were children in the film held a panel the day after my friends left town and talked about their experiences. They were elderly now. The West Texas desert felt powerful, the kind of female deity that we forget can exist: She's mean. She's boiling with anger. She killed Scalia right here just this past February.

It took me a week to find weed. I had flown out of California with some in my carry-on, which I've been told by a friend's attorney husband is completely legal, but I'd smoked it all with the women who were in town for the Lannan Residency. I went to a weirdo bar that served bad pizza but was literally the only place to get food in town since all the grocery stores were closed and it was a Tuesday.

At the weirdo bar I met a couple: she, fifty-two, he,

twenty-seven. They sold me the rest of their weed but only after they asked if they could fuck me in the bathroom. I said no, but when they asked for my number, I relented, because I wanted to stay in touch in case I needed more weed or got horny down the road. That turned out to be a huge mistake, since he wouldn't stop calling, and later, she left me a three-minute voicemail about her feelings about it. I hid out in the house I was renting.

•

Two weeks into my stay in West Texas, I began receiving messages from L, a young Egyptian Muslim woman living in the Midwest. She was in her twenties and living with her parents, and her father was abusing her mother.

I'd met L at a liberal arts college in Ohio months earlier, and we had clicked. She told me, in a faculty lounge with a cheap piano in the corner, that her parents had given her an "American" name so she could fit in, but that instead, she was hypervisible in her hijab. In Egypt, no one thinks of her as Arab, because of her name. In America, no one thinks of her as American, because of her hijab.

Our messages were short, clipped. She was feeling guilty, blaming herself for the abuse. I tried to help without sounding clueless, privileged. At some point, she told me she didn't want to call shelters or social workers who will give her white-women solutions. She said, "This isn't just abusive. This is Egyptian."

She said she had a hard time sleeping. That she'd been sitting in her closet, with the door closed, for privacy. That through the day and night, she could hear her mother wailing. L went from telling me her mother would never agree to go to a shelter to writing and saying that her mother was ready to move out.

I reminded her that she was over eighteen and had the right to live wherever she wanted. She responded that, while that sounded nice, how would she afford it? Here, L's problems all intersected: she was the daughter of an Arab immigrant, she was Muslim, she was a woman, she was young. Her future, she said, appeared dim. She corrected herself: "I cannot even see my future at all."

Two days later, she wrote to me and said she called the police. She said her mother was screaming and she couldn't stand by anymore. She was afraid to call the police on her dark-skinned Muslim father, but she felt she had no choice. When they arrived, they removed him from the house and promised L and her mother shelter. A few hours later, they said there was no shelter available to house her disabled sister. That night, the police allowed L's father back into the house.

Now L felt like a traitor, an untrustworthy and worthless person. I assured her she was not, that she was brave to report her father. She asked me, "How can a person call the police on her own father?" I told her, "The same way there can be a person who frightens and abuses their own daughter."

6

LOVE IS BODYSOME

My body was small; then it was not. That is the story almost all of us have about our bodies. At some point, we were infants, and, because we were fed and swaddled and because we slept, we grew. Our cells multiplied. We stretched. We expanded. I was the height I would always be by the time I was eleven. That is also when I began menstruating. My mother sat with me on my Ikea bed and told me I was a woman now. I didn't own any bras then.

We had a Quran in our house in Kuwait when I was growing up, but I rarely saw anyone reading it. In my house, adults read diet books. Adults followed diets ritualistically.

My mother had a large ass. I knew this because when she sat at the piano bench to teach music, children pointed at her ass and laughed. I knew this because my father told her she had a fat ass. I knew this because she sometimes walked around our apartment naked, her dimpled ass smiling, the apron of her belly flap forming a soft W under her belly button.

I thought all women's bodies were supposed to look like my mother's. My body now is its larger twin; I have a smiling, dimpled ass and a W of my own. But in photographs of her in the sixties and seventies, my mother looks different: smaller, doe-like, her hair long and straight. It's as though giving birth to my brother and me transformed her; it did. And she's spent her entire life since then trying to be that woman she was before she became a mother, trying to slim her way back to being A Girl. I dieted with her in solidarity. Except I was eight years old when I started; I was still A Girl.

No one stopped me. I didn't read the diet books, just aped and mimicked what my mother did. I drank soup for lunch. For dinner, I ate a piece of chicken. In the morning, I ate nothing. And then there were secret comforts. Home from school in the afternoon, I stood in our wide, blue kitchen and ate a bag of cheese puffs. Each puff was my friend. Each filled me, leaving its orange dust, its ashes, on my fingers. My mother did this, too. I saw her at odd hours in the kitchen, snacking. She made sexual sounds when she ate. Moaned at her mouth tasting something, at her body filling up.

In our family pool's changing room, white women, expats, walked around naked, their bodies like men's. That is what I believed, because their bodies were rigid, athletic, absent of the Ws and dimples my mother had. Their breasts were small and their nipples pink. I was confused by my body's reaction to them; I couldn't name arousal. At around this same time, I saw an ad in a magazine of Nastassja Kinski shampooing her hair. I masturbated to the ad, and to the seventies *Playboy*s my brother and I found in storage drawers in the dark sitting room reserved for guests.

In films and on television, I don't remember seeing white women eating. Arab women ate on Arabic soaps, and danced, and laughed. At home and in the kitchens of families and friends, women milled around the table serving us and then sat and ate with us; at home, my mother mostly milled.

The Cosby Show and *Roseanne* were on almost nightly, the Cosbys gathering and talking in their kitchen, usually standing up, the Conners sitting at their kitchen table even in the credits, a camera milling around them.

My mother was a chubby Clair Huxtable, chic in eighties skirts and blouses, dark-skinned, her hair done. My mother was also Roseanne, fat and loud and hungry.

•

When we moved to America in 1991, I weighed 104 pounds. I was thirteen and eating six hundred calories a day. I weighed myself after school. Then, I stopped weighing myself. I began checking my size by wearing a green pair of shorts, the pair of shorts I'd moved to the U.S. in, every night before bed. I was able to fit into these shorts until I was about fifteen. At that point, the shorts would zip up but not button. Then, when I turned sixteen, they stopped fitting.

I tried everything, but the shorts would not go up past my hips. I ate a slice of toast in the morning, an apple for lunch, and half a cup of pasta for dinner, dipping down to 450 calories, but the shorts still would not fit. I danced for an hour in my room every day. The shorts would not fit. I lay on my back and tried to zip them up that way. They would not fit.

Nothing I did would make it so that I was the same body, the same person, the Girl I was before I moved to the U.S.

My mother never explained to me that a fifteen-year-old is not a complete adult, that I still needed to grow. I didn't understand why my body was changing, and so I thought it was punishing me, rebelling against me. At this same time, my father was monitoring my every move very closely. And I wanted to be in control of my own body somehow. So I starved.

When starving stopped being fun, there were boys. Boys went in and out of me. But it was in college, my belly on the bed, my dry elbows propping me up, my mouth on the ridge of my friend L's pussy, that I thought: Oh. Is this what I've been hungry for?

•

Two months after my son moved out on his own, I met a new boo. It was difficult for me to have a boo when I lived with my son, because I wanted to be discreet, I wanted to maintain boundaries, I wanted to protect my privacy and his. Once he moved away, I was on my own for the first time in my life, and I was happy about this and about my new lover. He loved my breasts. Sometimes, he came over just to nurse. He would ask that I continue to do my work, as I normally would, and then he'd curl his six-foot frame into my loveseat, place a pillow under his cheek, and nurse my breast. He sucked and closed his eyes. I worked. When he opened his eyes, I blew gently at them, to close them again, something I used to do with my son. I didn't understand what this was: me nursing a man who was not my infant, who did not need me for sustenance. I nursed him, and every time he flicked his tongue against my chapped nipple, I felt useful and alive, wanted, and loved. It was all pretend.

•

I was an infant, and I was lying on my back. The room was dark, as though the pitch-black sky was indoors, thick around me. Maybe my diaper was being changed—my legs were lifted. Then, a pain, radiating between them. A burning. Like someone struck a match inside me. I screamed, but I'm not sure if I was comforted. And now, all these years later, my vagina hurts when I see someone in pain. A quick, radiating pulse zaps through my vulva, like a live wire. The darkness of the room is my memory, protecting me. The darkness is my mind, pulling the night in to save me.

My father said to me, years later, "When you were a

toddler, your mother once put a suppository in your vagina instead of your buttocks." "Oh!" I said. "Oh, I remember that! I remember that pain." "Yes," my father said. "You cried and bled. We took you to the emergency room. It was terrible. The doctor there wrote a certified letter that your hymen was not broken, and that you had had this accident, in case a future husband wanted to know." And this, somehow this last detail, is the one that shocked me the most.

Therapists later would question this story. How do you know it was a suppository? they asked. How do you know it was your mother, not your father? Your mother, not anyone else?

The fact is, I don't know. The fact is, I love my mother. The truth is, I want to believe it was an accident. My anger isn't just about the abuse that happened to me. It's also about those events that occurred directly afterward—the hospital visit to make sure my hymen was OK.

•

I nursed my lover on the loveseat. He pulled nothing from me, and he was satisfied. I imagined showing him, or any of the many people I've fucked, the letter from the Kuwaiti doctor. I'm a virgin, I would say. Look. This was what was most important to my parents, to my health provider, to everyone around me. That I was still a virgin at twenty months old. No wonder the night sky came through to my nursery.

7

DOUBLE MAGIC

"Everything, indeed, is at least double," Proust wrote in *The Captive*, the fifth volume of his classic text, *In Search of Lost Time*. Anne Carson has explored how the closeted lesbian character, Albertine, is a stand-in for Proust the writer's lover, Albert. Albertine becomes Proust's doll.

I was in the toys section at a drugstore because I saw a doll I wanted to give my friend R's daughter—he was a man I was in unreciprocated love with. I touched the plush doll, imagining that I was the daughter. And in that act, I became double. I was his daughter's giver of gifts and I was the gift. I was his daughter and I was his lover.

I bought myself the doll. I bought myself several dolls. Each came with a story. She was made of mime's gloves. She was an ice cream shop attendant. She was a small, swinging satyr.

When I was small, my father brought me a doll when he came home from one of his business trips. She looked a little like me: her fabric face framed with tight brown wool curls, large facial features, short. Sometimes, at night, I would beat her. I would slap her cheeks, pinch her arms, and pull her hair. I found her in a box the last time I moved. I kept her in the box. I am ashamed of what I did to her, my twin and my daughter. More recently, I took her out of the garage, put her on my desk, and gave her a friend.

•

Back in Fresno, I met my friends at a bar every Monday night after I taught a class. The night I bought the dolls from the drugstore, I brought them to the bar with me, and I smoked the cigarettes I had just bought. I told my friends about the dolls. I said that I had a realization at the drugstore that I didn't need to be a child to own dolls. That I had my own income now and could buy any doll I wanted. I told them how, as I stood in the aisle, I still thought I had to choose only one doll, even after I'd allowed myself to buy toys. It took a few minutes, I told them, but I bought all the dolls I wanted. They cheered. Later, when we paid our checks, they asked me if I would play with my toys when I got home. The possibility filled me up completely.

My therapist, a woman of color, and the first therapist who has ever truly helped me, was very happy about this turn of events. She did play therapy, had a room full of archetypal doll characters—a girl child, villains, students, mothers, mermaids, firemen, etc.—and said that she wanted to talk to me about the doll I used to beat up. She asked me not to feel guilty, that it was in fact very common for children who grew up in households like mine, where violence was daily, to lash out and beat other children, and that I should be proud that I took things out on a doll. I used to apologize to her, I told my therapist. I would hug her and say I'm sorry. As I told my therapist this, I cried. My therapist is Latina and Indigenous, and we first started crying together when I spoke to her about Palestine. She told me that my apology was more than most kids do to the living, breathing children they hurt.

•

My friend H once told me a story about what he called "the Detroit doll." This was a doll he had spotted in a window he passed every day after school on his way home. The doll, which was almost four feet tall, stood behind the glass.

He later learned that the people in the house had lost their daughter. She had been killed that year. He didn't know how. He only knew that they pretended the doll was her, and they put her in the window so she could view the world outside it. But it seemed to him that she was the thing to be viewed.

•

They dressed me up in white gloves, pink tulle, flowered prints. They brushed my curly hair straight. They gave me pretty shoes. I was to emerge a few minutes after company arrived. When I came out to the living room, everyone oohed and aahed. When I climbed down the steps, the oohs began earlier, and I was royalty. My mother and father expressed intense, contradictory feelings for me, protective, reproachful, domineering, and erotic. They dressed me up and tore me down. I was their doll.

•

Armando Reverón, an artist in the 1940s, made dolls. They were woman-sized and he used them as models for his paintings. Their skin was burlap sack, their features almost macabre. A review of his work in *The New York Times* later said that Reverón "expressed intense, contradictory feelings for them, protective, reproachful, domineering and erotic. Collectively they were a cross between a play group and a harem." He liked to punish his dolls, too. They had highly detailed clay vaginas. He made them clothes, gave each doll a name.

•

For years I only watched *Alice in Wonderland* until Alice's point of arrival in Wonderland. Later in life I thought this was because I may not have had access to the full film. As though the Wonderland section had been censored, the way most films I saw as a child were censored. Later in life I found the 1951 version, and I projected it onto the wall of the house I would soon be evicted from. And yet even then, thirty or more years after I'd first watched *Alice in Wonderland*, I stopped watching the film at the point when she reached Wonderland. It's the section when she's on her way, in transit to Wonderland, that I am most captivated by. Her growing and shrinking body, her large and tiny tears, her dress-covered limbs buoyed in water, water of her own body's making. And most of all, the scenes where she is crawling through a brown and red tunnel, the walls all around her raw and ridged, a vaginal canal through which Alice is squeezed and squeezes, through which she transforms and comes to life.

What happens to young women whose adolescent sexuality is controlled, whose bodies' every movement is surveilled? Exit strategies and maps. We draw them up and go over the routes. We try the exits sometimes, at our own peril, too, because it's worth it to know that exiting could work. This would be like someone pulling open an exit door on an in-flight plane just to make sure it worked.

Alice wore a uniform. Women with exit strategies often do.

•

In the forties, right after the war, French designers were running very low on materials, and this gave birth to the

Théâtre de la Mode—a traveling theater of fashion. Each couture piece was made miniature, and each doll was a third the size of a woman, and sometimes they even wore panties.

•

"When a woman gives [a doll] to a woman, it's the life they cannot have, it is their child, sacred and profane . . . Sometimes if [Robin] got tight by evening, I would find her standing in the middle of the room in boy's clothes, rocking from foot to foot, holding the doll she had given us—'our child'—high above her head." Djuna Barnes wrote this in *Nightwood*, which is based on her relationship with a visual artist named Thelma Wood, whom she lived with in Paris, and who'd given her a doll.

Side note: Barnes admits that, once, when she was interviewing James Joyce, whom she admired very much, she totally spaced out.

•

In Ancient Egypt, statue makers went from creating elite and royal statues to making working-class statues. All these were gradually considered dolls, for play. Like Armando Reverón's dolls afterward, they were made of wood, of clay.

•

My first crush on a girl may have been on Thumbelina. In her, I saw a sister, a diminutive lover, my mother, and then, myself. She was trapped on a lily pad with a frog who was unkind to her. She had been sold off by her community. She was tiny, insignificant.

I knew about Thumbelina because we had a book about her and a book on tape to go along with it. The tape would beep when I needed to flip the page. The voice of the woman who read the story was commanding, elderly, and informed.

I was probably five or six years old when I listened to the Thumbelina tape, thumbing my way through the book at each beep. Thirteen years later, I would have a child. And within me already were all the tiny eggs I would ever have; deep within me part of my child already existed. And because my mother had lost her mother just before I was born, my own motherhood was already a part of my identity. I mothered my mother. And I mothered my brother, who was born thirty months after I was, and who I patted and cared for at night when my parents went out, or in hotel rooms while we were traveling and while my parents were at dinner.

The origin story of Thumbelina, or Tiny, as Hans Christian Andersen tells it, is that an older woman wanted a child but couldn't have one. She went to a sorcerer and was given a seed to make her own child with; when she planted it, the seed blossomed into a tulip. And now the gayest moment of Thumbelina: the old woman kissed the petals of the tulip—two petals, to be exact—and out came Thumbelina. She was half the size of a thumb. A tiny, perfect, anthropomorphized clitoris.

As a child, I was drawn to the miniature nature of this perfect being, and to her tiny accoutrements: her bed was a walnut shell, her blanket, a petal. She took up almost no space at all. She was nothing like me and she was everything like me. If I mothered my own mother, who actually came first? I wanted to be like Thumbelina: born of no man. It was like Surat al-Samad, the verse of the Quran I repeated in class and before bed: God did not beget and was not begotten. As an adult woman, I feminize the Quran so that this part reads, She did not give birth and nor was She given birth to. Thumbelina, like the divine, is perfect, whole, and mighty. Her physical size is irrelevant. She is indivisible, above all others, and for the entire length of her story, she attempts to escape lascivious masculinity as embodied by both the frog and his mother. She is never penetrated and is finally able to get away from her captors, releasing into a world of other fairies. She will never give birth to any other. In the fairy tale, she finds a prince her size who also emerges from a flower. The rest of their people join them, emerging from other flowers. It's a marriage of clitorises in a magical kingdom of clitorises, the final touch being a pair of tiny wings bequeathed to Thumbelina, giving her complete freedom. In that buzzing, the story ends, her entire self transformed into an orgasming, climaxing queen.

•

The foil of Thumbelina was, is, Tinker Bell. The first time I saw Tinker Bell glide across our television, I fell in love.

Her tiny green dress and long legs, with pointed feet, shoes with large white pompoms, and the fairy dust trailing her signaled an otherness and an inaccessibility, as did her white skin. Her red lips. Her indigo blue eyes and black brows and lashes. Her jealousy. Her possessiveness.

Her moment with that mirror, realizing that her hips were large. This moment did not exist in the book version, only in Hollywood's. But it made me wonder if I was too much. Shorts and other pieces of clothing would fit me imperfectly. I wasn't fat yet, but I wasn't skinny. And seeing that even Tinker Bell, who could fly and was tiny, was worried about the size of hips, made me love her more. For a moment, I thought we were alike. I could relate to her.

All of this, and her unavailability, made me desire her deeply. I wanted to be her, and I wanted her to be mine.

Thumbelina and Tinker Bell are both, in my imagination, queer, visual representations of clitorises. They buzz, they yearn, they are tiny and hidden, and sometimes tiny and visible. They are wet. They flicker. They want. They make you want back.

•

For years after the 2006 Israeli war on Lebanon, whenever I wanted to conjure an image of a badass woman, I visualized a photograph taken just after ceasefire, of a store owner in flip-flops dusting off a white-wedding-gowned mannequin in the rubble outside her shop in Beirut.

•

I shared a room with my brother until I was ten. Those last two years, we pushed our beds together. Our mother was preoccupied with our little sister, who resembled a perfect doll—large eyes, beautiful cheeks. At night, my brother and I would play a game called mannequin. In this game, I would pretend to be a mannequin, singing a song I'd made up to complete my transformation, and he would explore my body. I would stay in whatever pose I had struck for several minutes, while he, then seven or eight, pushed my butt cheeks apart, tickled my belly. Then, he would become a mannequin, and it would be my turn.

When I told my mother about these games, she said that they happened because the devil was whispering into our ears, and that we shouldn't listen. I imagined a small, red, horned doll talking into my ear, and I didn't separate from my brother until one day, when I pushed my bed all the way to our study room and staked a claim on it as my own.

•

Barbies' blank vulvas fascinated my friends. We undressed the dolls and stared at their nothingness. I held my own secret obsession. I was in love with Barbie's arched foot. I could articulate her foot in three different poses. Putting the shoe on her foot and then peeling it off, putting it on, peeling it off. Licking her arch. It occurs to me now that the arched foot would have been a great toy to flick against my clit. But I didn't think of that as a child. I wish I had. And if Barbie were real, she wouldn't be able to carry her own weight. Online, one can find a chart of her measurements that shows this. Her feet are a girl's size 3. As a living woman, she would have to get around on her knees.

•

My friend R and I sometimes went to Suzy's, a local sex-toy shop, for fun. We giggled at the two-foot-long cocks, at their patriotic names—The Great American Challenge! I was taken with the hacked-up women's bits on sale—a silicone ass with a hole, a silicone pair of massive tits, a silicone vulva. Fleshlights writ large. Then there were the full dolls. I wondered if masturbating with them was satisfying. I was reminded of Barbie's tiny foot, all the erotics I once placed therein, on something so small when I myself was small. Sometimes I resented my vibrator for its lack of heat. Its veins were ridges without a pulse. And worst of all, it was not connected to a warm body. But I enjoyed watching it go in and out of me. The way people who own these dolls probably enjoy watching themselves disappear into them.

•

I once performed surgery on my Cabbage Patch Kid's belly-button, on a flight from Amman to Kuwait. With needle and thread, I sewed the button tighter. My father had bought me the doll in Italy, when we were all there together. I named her Jennifer. I didn't know I could give white dolls Arabic names. This was left over from the Enid Blyton books my British teachers assigned me. White families had picnics and wore coats. These books were like sci-fi to me. I loved Jennifer's belly button; it was a nipple, a clitoris.

My father now says that my Cabbage Patch Kid doll was the first one ever in Kuwait. But I preferred a cheap doll my mother and I had once bought from a market. The doll came with a bottle, and through a trick in the bottle's plastic, holding it up to the doll's lip made all the milk appear to be guzzled up, and it disappeared.

My nursing lover said his favorite thing was to watch his dick go in and out of my mouth. He said he loved watching it disappear in me.

My mouth was a magician.

8

A STREET CALLED CHESTNUT

Imagine my mother in 1977. She was twenty-four years old, and pregnant. She lived in Chicago, above a Wendy's, on a street called Chestnut. The street was just off Michigan Avenue, Chicago's Magnificent Mile. She was Egyptian, petite, long-haired, and beautiful. She was living apart from her family for the first time, and she was thousands of miles away. Her body had never been this far west. She stood at the window on the twenty-fourth floor of her apartment building and stared out at the city, and in the afternoons, she visited museums and went for walks on Lake Michigan. She spoke only Arabic and French, but she managed.

When my parents first arrived in Chicago from Kuwait,

they stayed at a hotel. My mother said she was lucky because she made a friend very quickly, Gh, a visual artist and a Palestinian. My mother and Gh spent days together. But my mother didn't boast of many or any other friends during this year, when she and my father were in Chicago so my father could do a one-year apprenticeship with a civil engineering firm.

"When I was hungry," my mother told me, "I would go downstairs and eat a biggie fry. From Wendy. I ate most French fries during my pregnancy."

My son and I are addicted to French fries.

In November of my mother's year in Chicago, her mother stopped calling from Alexandria. Her sister and father called, but they always claimed that her mother was sleeping or out or busy. My mother had her suspicions. When I was born in January and my mother's mother didn't call to congratulate her, my mother was more than suspicious. Soon afterward, my father and her family told her: my grandmother had died, of a massive heart attack, back in early November. All the strange letters my mother was receiving from her were actually written by my aunt, who was eighteen at the time.

Her family hadn't wanted to tell her because she was pregnant. The idea was that they needed to protect her pregnant body, and my unborn body, from the news, from the shock of grief. Ironically, my mother instantly plunged into a deep depression, which might have aligned with an ongoing postpartum depression, a depression that lasted five years or more. During her time in Chicago, she would stare out of the window of her apartment and wish she could jump. She wanted to slide the glass open, brave the cutting wind, and release herself. She says I saved her. That she would look at my infant body sleeping, or into my baby eyes, and wonder, who would take care of me?

Years later, in a sushi restaurant, we were a little drunk, and my mother said she thought I was her mother. That I am her reincarnation? I said, but my mother said, No, you are my mother.

•

My mother refused to visit her mother's grave, to confront the fact of her mother's body, buried. Of course—who can confront the fact of a mother's death? She moved back to Kuwait with my father, got pregnant with my brother. She gave birth to him when I was thirty months old. It wasn't until two years afterward, she said, that she accepted that her mother was dead. She didn't reveal to any of her new friends during this time period that her mother had died. She spoke of her mother as though she were still alive.

I have known this story my entire life. And my entire life, I have felt guilty for being the reason my mother couldn't grieve her mother's death when it happened. I've understood, of course, that it was her sister's and father's responsibility to tell her, but I couldn't help it—I felt responsible, too; my fetal body was to blame.

My visits to my mother's mother's grave are vividly and

indelibly rooted in my early childhood memories, probably because of the emotional turmoil my mother must have experienced to endure those visits. And the child's body is always so aware and so in tune with the mother's body. To its shifts and frequencies.

•

In the winter of 2007, two months after my then-husband moved in with me, we went to Chicago. His friends, two unbearable men, met us there. We would all walk through the city, visiting art museums and bars and diners. My then-husband's friend, a white Republican Zionist asshole whose social media profile praised the Israeli army, was sleeping on the foldout sofa in our hotel room. We spent a late afternoon walking from one part of the city to another, and I yearned to see the street on which my mother had lived, the first apartment building I had slept in, day in, and day out, for the first few weeks of my life.

At some point on our walk, we passed Chestnut Street. My then-husband was walking ahead with the Zionist, and his other friend was holding hands with his fiancée. I was trailing behind. Wanting a sense of connection, I shouted to them all, "This is Chestnut Street! Where my parents first lived when they moved to America! It's where I lived as a newborn!" No one cared. They were all white Texans, essentially; none had the faintest idea what it meant to be continually refugeed, constantly uprooted and hurried forward and off-ward, and they kept walking. Once, when my then-husband had brought me to visit his hometown, it took him less than fifteen minutes to show me his first house, his elementary school, his middle school, his high school, and the house he lived in until his high school graduation. I had jokingly said that it would take several weeks and thousands of dollars in airplane tickets for me to show him where I'd lived the first eighteen years of my life. Now, trailing behind him in Chicago, I walked slowly, hoping that having my feet on Chestnut Street would mean something, would affect me in some way. This was the first address I ever had, the first of dozens. But nothing happened, no quaking under my feet. I wanted to cry. Instead, I ignored all of them for the rest of the trip.

In the morning, the following day, I walked from the hotel back to Chestnut Street. I called my mother when I arrived and asked her the address of the building. She told me, and I walked to it, describing the street now, with its new restaurants and offices and businesses. When I got to the building, I told her I was there, and I described the entryway. She spoke animatedly and feverishly, excited that I had discovered it, perhaps relieved that that part of her life was real and true, that a building from her past still stood.

She asked me where I walked there from, and I said, "from my hotel." I casually mentioned the name of it. "The Allerton," I said. My mother burst into laughter. "The Allerton!" she said. "That was the hotel I stayed in before we found that apartment, when I was pregnant. I once did that same walk you just did, from the hotel to the building. We did it together!"

•

During my road trip in 2016, I was finally able to go to Chicago alone. Once I arrived, I drove straight to the house in Ravenswood where I would be staying with my dog. It was raining, and we ran through the rain, until I picked her up and we made it inside. The next day, the sun showed off, and we walked down to get pizza.

I drove out to the apartment my mother and father stayed in when they first moved to America. It's downtown, and there were tourists and locals walking in the sun, taxis, even a horse-drawn carriage, but I found parking, and I walked my dog up State Street to Chestnut. We stood in the front reception area, where a couple of Arab women held strollers with their own children in them. I wanted to hug them both, and even though they were younger than me, I wanted to tell them that in this moment, they were my mother, too. When I asked the doorman if I could go up to my parents' old apartment, he rang the current tenant, who declined a visit. This was to be expected—I only wanted to stand in the lobby with my dog and breathe and remember what it must have been like to be carried and swaddled by my mother, by my father, and the moments we stood in this same exact spot, bracing for the cold to come.

9

UNDERGROUND

In the house in Connecticut, we had a basement. The basement had a storage and laundry area to the left and a seating and video game area on the right, with a sofa bed, a cheap, plush corner couch, and a plastic table. When I was fifteen, my father began taking me down to the basement to teach me about what was acceptable and what was not. He and my mother had seen *Basic Instinct*, and in the basement, my father told me that it was shameful and wrong for a woman to be on top of a man during sex. Another day, he took me down there when he discovered that I was planning to go to a party, and he explained to me why girls shouldn't go to parties. One afternoon, he beat me in the basement because I was talking on the phone with a boy. Another night, he beat me in the basement, straddled me and choked me, and

I asked him to kill me. This frightened or confused him, because he stopped.

I used the basement to sneak out of the house and go to clubs and parties and on drives with boys. I would sneak down there when everyone thought I was sleeping, and I'd sneak back in at dawn. This worked for over a year. I was always terrified of being caught. The poetry of this secret exit from my family always appealed to me. It was a fantastical version of my friend L's basement apartment—I pretended I had my own realm. And it was the place where I was punished, and so, it was also the place from which I escaped.

•

My first memory of a basement is not of a basement at all. It's of our apartment in Kuwait during a monsoon. My mother had brought me back to the apartment after a short absence, and everything was underwater. I was almost knee-deep in it. I was five or six. Most memories of Kuwait are of sunshine. But this particular day was gray dark. Everything had a charcoal sheen to it. Especially the water. This memory haunts me because it's a foreshadowing of the Gulf War, which wouldn't come for another five years.

•

There was a cellar in Palestine, in the house my father and his brothers built for my grandparents. My parents and siblings and I visited the house every third summer. The cellar was where we kept the meat and sodas and milk and cheeses refrigerated. Its walls were charcoal gray, and light came in through the cellar door. My cousins and I sometimes went down there to sneak Coca-Cola. But the Coca-Cola was Israeli; I remember the letters in Hebrew. It was sweeter than any cola I'd had before.

•

When I was eight, my family moved to a new apartment in Kuwait, on the fourth floor of a blocky white building. Every floor housed a single apartment. There were four of these buildings, all in a square block, each with its own courtyard. My brother and neighbors and I would go look at the other versions of our building, the other versions of ourselves. One day, our neighbor Lana, who lived on the first floor, asked us if we wanted to see the basement. We thought she was trying to trick us. Watch, she said, and she stuck a key into the elevator on the ground floor, and we took the elevator down to the basement.

The basement was identical to all the other apartments, except it was not. It was a bachelor pad—the first one I'd ever seen. The giant living room had a pool table and a Ping-Pong table in the middle. The small living room was filled with blue seating. There was no kitchen. The bedroom was enormous and had a floor-to-ceiling poster—or maybe that's just how I remember it—of Marilyn Monroe in fishnets. I liked going to the basement just to see the poster. This basement apartment belonged to my friend L's brother, who was away in college. The poster and the bedroom and the entire basement belonged to him. Men got to have spaces. While my family at the very top floor had zero freedom, here was the basement, completely free.

When there were air raids and bombings, we would run down to the basement.

•

When I was sixteen, I snuck out of the Connecticut basement to see a boy I was dating, a seventeen-year-old aspiring DJ. He and his friends picked me up from the dead end of our street. They took me to clubs, we ate at a diner, and then we went to a river. He and I kissed and touched each other for hours. When he dropped me off at home, all the lights in the house were on, even though it was dawn. We knew I'd been caught. He offered to let me stay the night at his house. He said his mother would be upset but that she would understand. He said he was worried about me going in. To this day, I don't know why I didn't go with him, why I didn't choose snuggling next to someone who cared for me over punishment. I had never slept next to anyone I was attracted to before. I said no, and I kissed him goodnight. I snuck back in through the basement as usual, took off my clothes and put on the nightie I'd left down there, behind the sofa bed. The sounds of my father's and mother's feet thundering down the steps. And then it began.

Like rain lashing at a window. Like a flood. Like a doll cut up into five distinct pieces. Legs, arms, head. Like a cardboard box with a sword through it. Like a fist. Like a magnifying glass over something in large print. Like a clap.

My body, covered in red marks. My father slapped me, pulled my hair, punched my arms, which I hid my face behind. I was on my period. I bled and bled. My mother did nothing, always did nothing. I said, "I didn't do anything wrong." His one hand held both my small hands and his other hand knocked me against the side of my face, like a heavy bookshelf falling on my cheek. I ran upstairs. I wanted to emerge from underground. He ran after me. I ran out of the house, screaming. He chased after me.

I ran in a circle around our house. He ran in a circle around our house. No one called the police. Our neighbors on all sides were white. I was screaming. Not a single neighbor tried to help. My face was red and my tears covered my face. My father commanded me to go back inside. I don't know why I did. We were back in the basement. He was kicking me. He was on top of me. He was slapping me. Afterward he and my mother sat on the cheap corner loveseat and explained to me what life was. That there were rules. That I was a whore. They left calmly, now that all my father's energy had flashed out of him, like fire. Had burned me.

I waited a few minutes. Maybe twenty. Then, I ran. I opened the basement door to the backyard and ran, up the concrete stairs, down the street. I was in my nightie. I could have changed into my clothes, laced my shoes on, but I didn't want to change anything, didn't want to alter in any way the scene of the crime, which was my body. I ran down another street, all the way to the bottom, to a pay phone I used to use to call my friends. The pay phone was dead. I ran across the street to the hotel where my parents let guests stay when there was no room at our house, the fancy hotel. I ran to the front desk. I asked the woman there to call the police. She appeared inconvenienced. She called the police and said that a guest had been assaulted. I corrected her and said I was not a guest. I corrected her and said I ran to the closest place where I knew people would have to help me.

The police came. The police were two men, one Black, bald, and one white, young. They took me to a small, private office behind the concierge, a room that had white walls, a desk, and a telephone. I wondered, later, if that was where the hotel keeps the luggage of people who have to check out but don't have to leave until later. I only spoke with the Black police officer. The other one did and said nothing. The police officer asked me to describe everything that had happened. I did. He asked me if this happened to me often, my father beating me. I said it did. He asked me if he could take photographs of my red welts and marks. I said he could. He took Polaroids of the redness on my temples, the side of one of my cheeks, my legs, my behind. I was still wearing the baby-pink nightie.

I looked at the Polaroids and thought, That doesn't look like much. Just redness. My father never really left bruises. He never punched, just slapped. My head was covered in hair, so I couldn't show the police officers the redness there.

The police officer wanted to know where my family was from. I told him. He said, That is going to cause a lot of trouble for your father. My entire body stiffened, reddened again, as if I'd been beaten anew. The police officer said, Your father is an Arab and he's beating his child. That will be a real problem for him. I imagined my family having to move back to the Middle East. And where would they live? I imagined myself living in a foster home. Having to withdraw from college. I imagined my mother shamed, her husband in jail.

I don't want that to happen, I said to the police officer. I just want my father to stop hitting me.

The police officer didn't say anything that I can remember.

On the drive to the precinct, the police officer let me sit up front, and he smoked a cigarette. I asked him if I could have one, and he said yes. I lit the cigarette and stared ahead as he drove. Part of me wished this police officer could be my father. I was still barefoot.

At the precinct, I sat in a waiting room. I didn't know what would happen next, if I would be sent to be processed somewhere. I waited for hours. Finally, another officer came and said I was ready to be picked up. I sprang up and walked out to the front room, only to find that my mother was there, that she was the one picking me up. She signed for me, as if I were a package, luggage she didn't want, and I walked out with her, even though I was afraid to; I walked to our car. She said to me, pointing at my feet, that I would always be barefoot in life. This felt like a decree. I did not understand why it was me she was angry with. Why wasn't she angry at my father for beating me? For creating such stifling, unhealthy rules that disallowed me from doing anything at all? She drove me in silence, tried to guilt me about my father. I asked her if he was in jail. She said he was at home.

•

At home. I didn't understand. She said the police officers came and questioned him, and he invited them in for coffee, and they all chatted about how my father had a pristine record, and how I was a badly behaved slut, and how I chose to stay out all night, even though I was a minor.

I was a minor who went to college and read Balzac; I was a minor who had been beaten her entire life. Nothing mattered; I was not just a minor, I was minor.

At home, I changed, put socks over my dirty feet, and got ready to go to my job. I'd called and asked a coworker to pick me up. My father said nothing to me, except, in a disingenuously kind voice, that I could take my own car to work. But my car, I understood, and always had, was not actually my car, since I could only use it with permission. It was another way for my father to further imprison me, make me dependent on him. I left for work in my friend's car. I hadn't slept all night. I felt faint. From the middle of the store floor, I saw the register floating. I was hallucinating.

During my break, I walked down to S's job, which was four blocks away, and told him what happened that morning.

How my body hurt. He didn't react. It seemed as if he wanted me to leave. So I left. What I learned from this was that no one would ever want the burden of caring for me, of healing me, not for the next twenty years, not ever. I had to do everything myself. Later, I understood that we all do.

•

Twenty years after this incident, in Marfa, I looked up Connecticut laws regarding child abuse. The FAQ section of the website instructed people and witnesses to always believe the child—a child being anyone under the age of eighteen—and to never approach the parents about the abuse, but to report it directly to the Department of Children & Families, which works in tandem with officers to hear the child's own version of events, to fight for the child's rights to live in an environment without being in physical pain or emotional anguish, and to find that environment for that child, if necessary. None of those things happened for my child self.

A month after I reported my father to the police, the three of us—my father, my mother, and I—were due in court. The day of the hearing, my father dropped us off at the courthouse and drove off to find a parking space. My mother and I sat on the steps and waited. The irony of this moment never occurred to me, sitting there, waiting for my abuser to join me. There was a puncture in each one of us. Except there was no light coming in.

When he was several yards away, my mother and I

watched my father walking up the hill in his suit. Look, she said to me, Look at him walking. He hasn't slept in days. He's been pissing the bed. I watched him walk, as she told me to. I imagined urine dripping down his expensive trousers. I owned two pairs of jeans. I turned to my mother. In that moment, she succeeded. I felt guilty about my father leaking.

I had been told that once I arrived at the courthouse, the first step in my case, our case, was to climb down the marble steps . . . to the basement. In the courthouse's basement, we waited for an hour and then were "separated"—we should have never carpooled and then sat together as a unit to begin with, as the case wasn't the state vs. us but myself vs. my father. A child welfare worker sat me at her desk and asked me questions. Did my father hit me? And what was I doing that night? How many boys had I had sex with? Did I think it was a good idea to leave the house in the middle of the night to have sex with boys? Where did I think such behavior would lead? She didn't ask this last question, but in my memory, she might as well have: If I was going to behave like such a whore, why was I surprised to come home and be treated like one?

That was really it. I don't recall anyone asking me if I wanted to press charges, only that I did not want to press charges. I didn't want my father to be deported. I didn't want my mother and siblings to suffer. We climbed up the steps, and my father stood in the front of the courtroom with other defendants on the docket and a public defender. My mother and I stood in the back. Soon afterward, the case against my father was dismissed, because I didn't testify or press charges, and he walked up the courtroom's aisle, a groom of anguish, and we walked out into the street.

His name appeared in the town's newspaper that week. In the police blotter section. There were no details, only that police had gone to his home, and the date and time that they did. When I saw it, I felt a grim satisfaction that the only time my father's name appeared in our local paper was because of what he had done to my body; it was because of me.

Though the law and those who were charged in implementing it failed me, my father must have understood that if I were to call the police again, he would certainly be arrested, or more. Because, in the short years that I was forced to live with or near him after this event, my father never hit me again.

10

WHAT LOVE IS

The first time he hit me, I thought it was by mistake. As if throwing a woman against a wall was the same as accidentally breaking a glass or scratching a bumper against a steep curb. Besides, I'd grown up seeing my mother beaten, so I thought that maybe, just maybe, this was what love was.

The second time he hit me, something felt off. It helped that he did it in public. We were at a clothing store in the Village, and a throaty, tough woman, her Queens accent a bright mockingbird, told me I didn't have to live that way, that I didn't have to let him talk to me or touch me like that. I wanted to climb into the pockets of her thick coat.

I could have stayed in the store and refused to go home with him. I could have called someone and asked them to help me—but who? My mother didn't know I was dating anyone—I wasn't allowed to have a boyfriend, anyway, at seventeen—and I knew everyone else would advise me to just break up with him. But I wasn't ready. Not yet. I hadn't had enough.

If I didn't call him every night to tell him where I was—I was usually just in my dorm room—he would show up without notice and rough me up. There were also things that confused me: bouquets of flowers and nice dinners and candles. Plus, the sex. The sex was good.

The third, fourth, fifth time he hit me, I understood. That he would always find something small I'd done or said and punish me for it. That days later, he would always do or say something big to apologize.

He was my thirteenth lover. Now, looking back, thirteen lovers by the age of seventeen seems like an exaggeration. But I was in a race against time, against my father. If I could have sex with as many people as possible, I could remove myself as far away as possible from his grip. Somehow, this delivered me right into someone else's grip, and their grip was crueler than my father's. It left bruises. At least my father loved me—or was supposed to.

You're thinking I left this guy soon after. That it was a foolish, rookie, college girl mistake. But no. I stayed with him. I married him. I had his baby.

He wasn't the first cruel lover I'd had. When I was fourteen, a boy in my high school—we'll call him S—sexually assaulted me at his house and I didn't know who to tell. A year later, when I decided to lose my virginity, I picked him.

It made perfect sense to me at the time. He was not a gentle first lover. Although I gave consent, memories from the first time I had sex always come back to me painfully, the way memories of an assault would.

I recently looked S up and found out that he is a Connecticut police officer. When I googled his name and the words "police officer" while I was writing this, to see whether he was still a police officer, articles came up about how he was recently arrested for assaulting his wife and pulling her, by the hair, around their home.

I have an adult son now. Sometimes he is the only reason I refuse to believe that all men are hair-dragging maniacs.

Even when, and especially when, I look at his face and see some of the features of his father.

•

I was out with my college roommates when I met D. He was wearing a white T-shirt tucked into some booty jeans. His hair was slicked to the side. He looked like Johnny Depp if Johnny Depp were brown and a meathead.

D walked straight to me. He asked me questions. He put out a small fire I had accidentally started in my hair, where I had ashed the cherry off my cigarette. He hit me against the head a few times until the fire was out. I found a man who hit me within moments of meeting me. I was good.

He didn't come to my dorm room that night but took my phone number. A few days later, he called and showed up at my dorm with flowers; some nights, he threw pebbles at my window and told me to come down and took me to dinner. He went down on me like he'd found heaven between my legs. He spoiled me with his tongue and his affection.

He lived in a basement apartment in Yonkers. He drove me there all through that autumn, in his red Camaro. The basement was a few flights down, with a kitchen area to the left and a bedroom on the right. The bathroom was across the unfinished part of the basement, in which he'd set up his weights. That part of the basement apartment was the most eerie. The living space was warm and sexy; the other space was dark and filled with metal, with heaviness.

He licked between my legs and then we had sex for hours. I'd stay the night, my cheek against his chest. When I woke up, I'd have a rash all across my face, because he shaved his chest. He took me to breakfast, always took me to breakfast. He was a bouncer at a bar. He worked hard. He wanted to be smart. He was twenty-seven.

I was seventeen.

•

I'd lied and told him I was eighteen. Then, one night, after we'd smoked weed together and gone to a diner, I slid my license across the booth to him. He looked at my date of birth.

"Oh, well," he said. It did not at all faze him.

I lit a cigarette and waited for my disco fries.

•

One afternoon, it snowed. He came and picked me up from my dorm. On the way to his apartment, the car hit a patch of ice and we circled around once. He righted the car and kept driving. I was terrified and told him so. He was calm, said he'd been driving in snow for years.

When he called my dorm room and I didn't answer, he was upset. He wanted to know where I was. I'd tell him. Then, when he called and I hadn't told him where I was, he'd show up to the college. He'd find me wherever I was, kiss me, tell me he was worried. I'd kiss him back.

I went down to the Village with my friends one afternoon and got my nose pierced somewhere off of MacDougal Street. The stud I chose was tiny, with a flat turquoise at the tip. I had always loved turquoise. My mother and other North African mothers used it to ward off the evil eye. The needle going through my nostril felt like fire, but the pain was so quick I admired it.

I remember my ears being pierced, in a marketplace in Kuwait, a kind of bazaar. My mother took me when I was around two. She hadn't been able to pierce them when I was a newborn, which was customary in her family and her city, because we'd been in Chicago. I remember liking the place. I sat on a chair, and a man I didn't know punctured me. He held a gun to my earlobe and hurt me. I remember the sound of the piercing, the pain inside and outside my ear. The earrings were gold hearts. I wore them for years.

D liked my nose ring. He had tattoos and enjoyed pain, too.

During this time, my parents would pick me up every Friday and take me to their house for the weekend. That was the only way they could agree to let me live on campus. They thought college students only had sex Friday through Sunday. I didn't understand why they wanted to spend so much time with me. Most people my age had parents who couldn't wait to get rid of them. My parents seemed to be obsessed with me.

My parents were obsessed with me.

When I showed up with the nose piercing, my mother said my father would not like it. I ignored her. I was scared of my father seeing it, but I felt that my nose was mine. At dinner that night, my father said nothing. In the morning, he said nothing. In the afternoon, I asked him if he liked my nose ring. He said I was disgusting, and that if I didn't take the stud out, he would take me out of college.

I went down to the basement and started my laundry, tried to ignore him. I watched television with my sister. I heard my parents rustling around upstairs, their footsteps going from my bedroom to theirs. They called me up to them.

When I went up, my father was lying in bed, holding a picture of D I had photocopied. I had tucked the image into my backpack's front pocket. He asked me who the man in the picture was. I said it was a picture I'd copied from a magazine. Then he took out a bag of weed from his pocket. My bag of weed. I had forgotten it in a flannel shirt I'd taken off in my room. He asked me when I started smoking. I said the weed was my roommate's, and that I'd taken it from her because she was a pothead. Then, he took out my birth control pills. He asked me how long I'd been taking them. I said I'd started taking them two months ago to regulate my period. The entire time I spoke, I remained calm. I did not want to be taken out of college. The aid I was receiving wasn't enough for me to go without my father's financial support, and he knew that and lorded it over me.

He smirked. He didn't give back any of my things. I asked for the birth control pills. He gave them to me, then asked me to go to the bathroom and take out my nose stud.

I stood in front of the bathroom mirror and, crying, twisted the stud until I'd taken it out of my nostril completely. I washed my nose. I washed my face. I kept the stud in a jewelry case for years afterward.

A few weeks later, I went back to the same place off MacDougal and got my navel pierced. This was the most painful thing I had ever experienced. A woman in a tank top and a bandanna clamped the skin above my belly button. She brought out a silver needle that resembled a rod. She sterilized my skin, asked if I was ready, then plunged the silver needle through. I had picked out a gunmetal-colored ring with a crescent moon and a star holding the ends together. She threaded that through the top of my navel and locked it into place.

The following weekend, my mother saw the navel ring as

I was coming up the stairs from the basement. She shouted at me, asked if I was trying to damage my body. It was strange for her to ask this, since she had stood by while my father had beaten my body so many times. I said to her, as calmly as I could, "It's my body."

"No," she said, screeching. "It's *my* body."

A few months earlier, she had found, in my closet, a pack of weight-loss pills. She'd confronted me about this, calling me a whore for being on birth control. I assured her that I was not having sex (I was) and that the pills were essentially ephedrine. She checked the labeling and asked her pharmacist and came back to me, relieved. "You're right," she must have said, "these are just weight-loss pills." And she gave them back to me.

I try to imagine that scenario now. If I found weight-loss pills and not birth control pills in my hypothetical daughter's closet, I would completely lose my shit. I would hug her; ask her why she thought her strong body needed to be made smaller. I would be thrilled if I found birth control pills, because she would be taking care of her body. This is all assuming I would rifle through a daughter's closet to begin with.

•

The most vivid diet my mother put me on is one where I ate nothing but pineapple and watermelon and strawberries all day, because of their supposedly enzymatic, scrubbing qualities. At night, I would sometimes get a hamburger patty. I vomited bile, pregnant with nothing but the possibility of my fatness. Over one summer, I had gone from 168 pounds to 140. Men paid attention to me. White men wanted to date me.

But I was still seventeen, and my mother was telling me that my body was hers. Because ownership of the child's body belonged to the parent. I'm sure that is how it was with her mother, her father. I cannot find any other way to explain or understand why she said this to me.

•

I got to keep the navel ring. My father never saw it. One night, having sex with D, it fell out. I waited a few weeks, then had it re-pierced. I called D from a pay phone afterward to tell him where I was. He was angry that I'd gone to do something without his permission, and he told me to get on the next train back to Yonkers. As I stood on the sidewalk, the receiver against my ear, I felt as though I were talking to my father.

•

When he picked me up from the train station, he was apologetic and kind. I didn't want to have sex that night, so I asked him to take me to my dorm. He wouldn't. I slept in his basement apartment, and in the very early morning, almost at dawn, he drove me on his motorcycle, my arms tight against his waist. I saw a classmate walking through the college gates, back to her room. She was a stripper in the city; I'd always admired her for that. It was how she supplemented her income and paid for part of college. I never felt that I could be a stripper, could never own my body so fully that I could make a living from it, charge people to look at it, have no shame over doing any of it. I desperately wanted to be a typical, normal college student again.

I climbed into my own bed and wept.

•

Things got worse. D demanded that I call him and let him know where I was if I was ever out of my dorm room after nightfall. If he called and I didn't answer, and he hadn't been told where I was, he would show up on campus to find me. One evening, I went out to dinner with my friends, and I called him from a pay phone at the restaurant to let him know where I was. He screamed at me. A few minutes later, while my friends and I were still waiting for a booth, he showed up; screamed at me in front of the waitresses, diners, and my friends; pulled me by the hair; and took me to his car.

I wanted out. At his basement apartment, I told him I didn't want to see him anymore. He said he would contact my father and tell him all about what a whore I was. That he had proof—photos of me, items of my clothing. When I cried and begged him not to do that, he pinned me against the wall and told me not to ever go out without asking him again.

It was worse than with my father.

•

He bought me flowers. He took me to dinners. He cried and held me and told me he was sick and that he loved me. He said that he always felt abandoned by his birth mother, whom he'd never met, and whose name he didn't know. He invented histories for her. She was a First Nations woman in Canada. She was a waitress in New Jersey. She was a house-wife in Connecticut. He said he would never hurt me again.

At a movie-rental store a few days later, he lifted a video up and asked what I thought, and I nonchalantly said that I'd read how the actor had to bulk up for the role. He squeezed my hand so hard it later bruised and walked me out of the store, into his car, and slapped me twice, hard, for talking about another man's body. If I appeared to be staring at a man on the street, he slapped me. If he saw that my blinds were drawn open at my dorm, he would slam me against the wall and ask me why I wanted other men to see me change.

•

When I was eleven, twelve, fifteen, I would lock the door to my bedroom and dance, lip-synching, pretending. I didn't know yet what a drag queen was, but my dream was to lip-synch and perform on small stages. Stadiums seemed too daunting. I dreamed small. I wanted wigs and makeup. I wanted short tutus and hose and to color my hair. I wanted my own body to be my own body. Whenever my brother or mother knocked on the door and told me to open up, I would lie and yell, "I'm changing!"

•

But I was changing.

And being with D, I changed again. I became less talkative. On campus, I often drifted off during seminars. My friends disliked him, wanted to know why I was still with him. I was afraid of him, and I was afraid of my father. I knew my father would take me out of college if he found out I had a boyfriend, someone I was involved with sexually, and I didn't know how I would finish college without his financial support. I was essentially trapped between an abusive man and a very abusive man, but I had no concrete way to verbalize this or to even recognize it.

I was at work at the diner when the O. J. Simpson verdict was announced that fall. I clapped, and my boss, the Greek owner of the diner, made a face. He was filled with sadness. I was siding with Simpson because he was a person of color. Because the Rodney King beating had happened right after I'd moved to the U.S. Because my family told me not to be involved in politics, to squeak by on my light-skinned privilege. And my boss was second-generation. He believed that

Simpson had murdered his wife. He believed that Simpson had battered her for years. He believed that Simpson should have faced proper justice.

And although we all had email at this time, there were no handy links on domestic violence for my friends to share. No social media to reach out on. No top-ten lists of red flags to watch out for. It was the nineties, and Snoop Dogg was saying that bitches weren't shit but hoes and tricks, and I was locked up in my room, dancing along. And hadn't my mother martyred herself and survived? My father beat her when he liked. She never complained, and in fact, she always spoke about how much she loved him.

That was what love was.

•

In February of 1996, D and I had unprotected sex, and I became pregnant. I remember cooking him a meal the night this happened, and he came home, saw me at the stove, then peeked his head out of the front door to check the address. Am I at the right place? he joked.

He held me from behind and covered me in kisses. He was affectionate and kind and he hadn't hurt me in weeks. After we ate the pasta I cooked, we got in bed, stayed there for hours. He was tender toward me and came inside me. I never came with D, except once, the first two weeks we were fucking, because I was tied to the foot of his bed and he was eating me out.

I was still working at the diner. D drove me there in the morning, and I walked to campus after my shift. The road to the college was green and leafy and windy, and I listened to a cassette on my Walkman. At my dorm room, I changed out of my diner clothes and read my art history assignments, started writing a paper. I know that this day didn't happen the day right after D got me pregnant, but in my memory, it does. I felt nauseated. I stood up from my desk and went to the bathroom, which I shared with M, my suite-mate. I vomited, but all that came out of me was bile. I knew I was pregnant.

Fear: that was all I felt for a while. On the weekend, out in Connecticut, I stole a pack of pregnancy tests from CVS and peed on all the sticks, and they all came up positive. I called my high school best friend and asked her to drive me to the hospital because they administered free blood pregnancy tests.

D picked me up that night and noticed the Band-Aid on the inside of my left arm, in the crook of it. He knew right away and became furious. He slapped me and told me I was a liar for getting a test without him. He dragged me out of his apartment by my hair and threw me down on the front lawn. I got up, terrified, and thought of walking back to my dorm room, but he grabbed me by my clothes and brought me back inside.

The next time I went to work, I looked through the yellow pages for an abortion clinic and called, made an appointment. But in bed every night—and D insisted that we spend every night together—D told me to keep the baby. He said that every woman he had gotten pregnant had gone to get an abortion behind his back. This didn't click for me at the time, that he wasn't supporting their decisions to terminate the pregnancies. It didn't occur to me, at all, that he had forbidden them from getting abortions. And it didn't occur to me, then, that he had gotten them, gotten us all, pregnant on purpose.

•

Reproductive coercion is what people call it. What happened to me has a name. A label. For years, I have felt only shame about my cowardice, about the fact that I didn't really want my baby, not until he was born.

•

Then, when I was about seven months pregnant, I bumped into a friend of my mother's at the clinic. Tante V was Egyptian—like my mother—and had lived in America for more than twenty years. I called her Tante, Egyptian French for "aunt." She had struggled with cancer for as long as we'd known her.

I understood why she was there. Routine blood tests.

And she understood why I was there. My belly was enormous. I was waiting for the results of a glucose test.

Tante V asked me where my mother was. I wanted to

tell her that my father had stopped talking to me when he found out I was pregnant, and that my mother was supposed to do likewise. She still called and took me out for burgers and gave me an old purple jumpsuit she wore when she was pregnant.

But I didn't tell her any of this. Instead I said that my mother was probably at home.

Tante V smiled at me. I could tell that it exhausted her to talk, and even to smile.

We got our test results at the same time. Tante V asked me if I wanted to come over to her house for lunch before driving back to my apartment in Yonkers. I agreed.

She lived in a pretty but modest home in the woods in Connecticut. Her kids had gone to prestigious private schools there. Her house was cold, as it was every time I visited. She always wore thick socks and sweaters indoors. I loved the cold of her house. My parents' house was always too hot. They turned the heat up so high that my hair and skin dried out all winter and I couldn't breathe.

Tante V was tall and very slim, and her movements were always slow and coordinated. It never occurred to me that chemo had contributed to her physique. I sat in her sunroom and ate a pasta salad as she made tea. She spooned sugar into my mug and then wiped her palms on her pants. This inelegant move surprised me, and I liked her for it.

Before I left, Tante V asked me when my baby shower was.

I was silent. No one was giving me a baby shower. My college friends had classes and lived in dorms. My mother couldn't give me one because she wasn't supposed to be talking to me.

"I will give you a baby shower," Tante V finally said.

•

A few weeks later, a friend picked me up to take me to the shower. I wore a black outfit I bought at Sears on sale. It had a pretty red bow, which sat at the top of my belly, so that I resembled a present to myself.

When we arrived at Tante V's house, balloons greeted us. Inside, it was uncharacteristically warm, and a caterer had left delicious food on the dining room table. My mother and some of her friends sat in the living room. One of my friends from high school showed up. But Tante V was missing. My mother told me she was not feeling well and was lying down in her bedroom.

I went up to say hello and thank her. She was in bed, looking pale and in pain. She hugged a blanket against her small belly. She didn't speak. I sat with her for a few moments until she shooed me away and told me to enjoy my shower.

The presents were better than I expected: a stroller with a built-in car seat. A highchair. Onesies galore.

The cake, blue and yellow, was my favorite part. It was in the shape of a baby over a moon. No one had bought me a cake in years, not since the last time my father let me have a birthday party. He disliked the chaos of birthdays and banned them at our home following the mayhem of my eleventh.

Tante V's living room was covered in gift wrap, and my mother took a photograph of me in the middle of it. Soon the caterers left, my mother rushed home, and my friend loaded my gifts into her car.

In all the excitement, I almost left without saying goodbye to Tante V. But before I could gather my things, she came downstairs to her sunroom. Maybe the festive mood in her house reminded her of when her boys were little or of a time before her illness, because she was smiling. She asked if I'd received good presents, things that I could use.

I told her I had. I wished I could give Tante V something in return, something that she could use. Perhaps sensing my sadness, she reached over to me, and I embraced her, my baby between us.

•

I gave birth via C-section. The anesthesiologist gave me an epidural, not a spinal block, and I ended up feeling a lot more pain than I should have. I have written my experience of childbirth as fiction over and over. I read Toi Derricotte's memoir-poem of childbirth in the West Texas desert. At the end of it, her son reads the book and says he didn't know she suffered so much. My spine warms and radiates at the point where that needle went in, almost twenty years ago, every time I experience a sense of assault, or deep fear, or physical vulnerability.

•

My son nursed quickly in the small room off to the side of the OR, where my body convulsed with pain. I felt comforted by his nursing, but I was still weeping and terrified of the pain I was experiencing. He'd been covered in goo when he was born, and was dark, as dark as my grandfather. He had black hair and a beautiful nose. His feet were crunched and I was worried about his toes. I wept and shook from fear and nursed my new baby. I asked that he be kept near me in the room I would eventually stay in. D either did or didn't spend the night that night. He went out to celebrate and I didn't see him again until morning. On the third day I wheeled myself to the shower and washed myself. My hair was long and knotted and felt impossible to unknot. I stopped trying. My body was still heavy and puffed as if it were still carrying my baby. Every few hours a nurse came in to wipe down my bleeding vagina and give me a new thick pad to lie in. I had a catheter and could slightly feel it on my urethra. I nursed my son and did not want to leave the hospital, ever.

•

When we left it was snowing and I was terrified of caring for my son under D's abuse. I hoped he would not continue to hurt me now that I had given birth to his child. I hoped that he would help me, as the doctor and nurses reminded us both that I was not supposed to walk long distances or carry anything heavy for thirty days. I hoped that things would be different, and they were. The sky was filthy dishwater and we had to stop at CVS because D hadn't prepared the house at all; we had no diapers, no baby wipes, no balms or blankets, nothing a baby would need. When we got to the apartment D behaved as though the baby seat was a constant obstruction, as well as the baby. I didn't own any maternity bras. I nursed and afterward I wadded up some tissue to absorb the leaks from my nipples. I changed the baby and burped the baby and held the baby and loved the baby. D picked up the baby once and said he stank. I wanted to ask him to give the baby a bath but was afraid. We bathed him together. I felt as though I were hallucinating the baby and the bath and D. I was on Percocet, and it was the only thing keeping me alive. D would go out every night, and a week after I gave birth, I went to the grocery store. I took the baby with me. I carried him and the groceries back into the apartment with me, as though there were no possibility of my abdomen coming open like a broken zipper on a skirt. I cooked dinners and ate what I could. I was always hungry and nursing. A month later D took me out. We went to the Met in Manhattan with another couple. I looked at the Ancient Egyptian statuettes and longed to feel mighty.

•

A few weeks later that couple found out that they were pregnant, and the woman, only a year older than me, had an abortion. I was struck with the sense of envy I felt. That it was so easy for her. That no one had threatened to kill her if she had an abortion. My son was six weeks old and his father was almost never home. I went back to school, filling my bra with toilet paper between classes while D's mother and father watched the baby. Sometimes I took my son with me to class. D's father drove me to and from campus, a distance that I could have walked, but it was winter, and D's father was kind.

•

Four months. I raised my son with D in the apartment for four months. D would shout when my son woke up to nurse, saying to keep him quiet. I did everything. D would go out and drink and come home and sleep for four hours, then go to work. This became the routine, every day. I didn't have access to a car. It was winter, Yonkers cold and dreary and wet.

My friend J would drive over from college and help me with the baby. She was there one day when D was home. D started a fight with me. I don't remember what it was about, only that he wanted to antagonize me. I was holding the baby. J asked if she could hold the baby. I handed him to her; he was warm, and small, and D slapped me, then pushed me against a wall and into a closed door. I tried to fight back but he kept hitting me. J took care of my baby and didn't get involved. I managed to get to the phone in the kitchen and called 911. He grabbed the phone from my hand and told the operator that I was stupid and hung up. Police showed up a few minutes later. They asked D to give me his keys and leave but didn't arrest him. He left with them, his key on the kitchen table. I lay next to my son and slept the deepest sleep I'd slept in a year. At dawn, D came back in with a second key he'd kept and mocked me for thinking I could keep him out of his own apartment.

•

In early spring, I went for a walk and noticed, a few blocks away, D's car in a random driveway. A few days later, he told me he had found someone else and was leaving me.

•

I moved into my parents' basement. D would try to harm me, to harm us, over the next few years, but we moved farther and farther away from him after that first move underground. It was over. I was free. I was safe. It was over.

Years later—my son an adult, my body much larger than it was when I gave birth to him—I sometimes received ineffable messages from my spine, from the part where the needle went in. My body remembers the needle. It remembers the months I spent carrying my child. It remembers my son's father kicking it. It remembers my own father's eyes on it, watching it move farther and farther away. It does not remember my mother's hand caressing it. At this time, I am unsure whether or not she caressed it. Perhaps I am mothering myself as I write by imagining my mother caressing this part of my spine.

This is the part of my spine that was meant to go numb. This small section of my spine that was sunk with a syringe and meant to fall asleep. Instead it woke up and is an insomniac. Its eye is wide and glassy, cracked, and aches in a broken and burning exposure. My son was pulled out of my uterus after the doctor cut a slit at the bottom of my abdomen, stretched my skin, took out some of my organs, arranged them on a metal tray nearby, cut open the sac where my son was growing, and pulled him out of me. I felt the pressure of the pull, my body not wanting to let go. I no longer feel that pull now, nor the pain at the bottom of my abdomen. The scar, from the cut and the stitching, is still numb. This is why my body believes I gave birth to my son through my spine. And this strength is also why I now believe that my body is all mine.

11

YES, GODDESS

When my son was about four years old, D was shot several times by a new girlfriend, a woman he'd met in Vegas. D was hospitalized and unable to walk for weeks. His mother called and told me, and I cried; she thought it was because I still loved him. My son was in the tub, in the trailer in Kyle, Texas, and I was watching him play with bubbles. I sat on the lid of the toilet, which, when we first moved in, I was forced to keep shut with several thick books. The previous tenant had found a rattlesnake in it the night she moved out.

D's mother listened to me sob about her son while my son bubbled in the bath. I was sobbing because my entire body had flooded with two griefs: one for my son, whom I would have to give the news to if D succumbed to his gunshot wounds, and the other for my old self, who had wished, and hoped, and done so with a feverish desperation, for a moment as liberating, as justice-delivering as this.

His girlfriend had been signing all the child-support checks that were mailed to a close-by post office box—I didn't want D to know where I lived. She had called me a few weeks earlier and asked me if D had ever hurt me. I said he had, and she described how he'd smashed her head against a windshield. She said she was in a motel and that she missed her horses. A few days later, she went back home. I hadn't heard from her since then. It wasn't difficult for me to imagine what he'd done to push her to protect herself. She was friends with all the police officers in her town. She could have reported him, but instead, she put a few caps in his ass (or, you know, his back) and got away with it.

Fourteen years later, I found the woman D had dated right after me. She had a child with him, too, and I wanted our children to be in touch. When we talked on the phone, she told me that for years she couldn't feel safe with a man. Any man. And that the man she married after she got away from D was so safe and kind that she ended up feeling no connection with him. I could relate. My second husband was the same way. I've searched for D's other girlfriend, the one who shot him, all over social media, but I have never found her. In my mind's eye she is on one of her horses, her pistol smoking.

●

I was still in Marfa, where I began taking countless selfies on Pinto Canyon Road, a country highway with almost zero traffic. Against the yellow background, my body stood in relief, a hieroglyph. The vastness of the sky, how the blue body of it snaked all around and above: Westerns began to make sense. The hubris of white men began to make sense. For what was this landscape but a canvas to swing a dick around in?

•

I've often returned to a favorite memory of my body.

I was walking down the street in a bathing suit. I was in Egypt, on my way to the beach. I was carrying the chair I would sit on when I finally reached the sand. I was a child, a girl. I was a girl child. No one commented on my body. No one said a thing to me. I was a light-brown noodle with feet and long hair. I was dry; soon, I'd be wet. My damp body would walk back to our apartment, invisible.

If Ramadan was in the summer, I'd watch a television show about the Prophet Muhammad. In scenes where he was present, his body and likeness were never shown. When he entered a room, a curtain billowed. When he moved something, it rose, unbidden, floating. For a long time, I thought the Prophet Muhammad's gift was invisibility. Later, religion teachers told me his gift was the word. But words are easy, I remember thinking. The ability to never have your body appear and still be powerful; that's hard.

•

Raahat el-binit, adults would say when a girl was no longer a virgin. "The girl is gone." The girl has vanished. This means she's a woman, no longer a girl. Where has the girl gone? Does sex automatically make a girl a woman?

I met with a young journalist, Y, while I was in Boston for work. We had drinks at a bar full of white men. Y was raised in a conservative Muslim community. When she decided to move out of her parents' home and to take off the hijab, which she had worn for years, her parents had said, Gone, the girl is gone. Y told me how difficult it was for her to be in a newsroom as a woman of color. How she was having sex with a Jewish guy who doesn't text her back.

I told her about my favorite fuckboi, the programmer in the Air Force Reserves. This was before he broke up with me, before the cabin in Washington State, when I still had him. I told her I was fucking him because he loved to kiss me, because he loved my large body. He would cup my right breast in his hand, my breast overflowing out of his palm, and he would remark on how beautiful my breast was. He would say he loved the ridges of my nipples. He would say that the peach color of my nipples was beautiful. He would point out the minuscule, barely visible pores, and talk about how perfectly structured they were: a grid in my skin.

I would imagine him programming drones, seeing the grids of homes. I would shout at him, later, in the kitchen, about this. He would say he did not program drones, but technical and boring things on airfields and cargo ships to keep people safe. And it has really come to this. There are so few men who enjoy kissing, who are good at it, who will kiss me the whole time we are fucking. Who will make me think, I feel as if I'm in love, but I know I'm not. And what's the difference? While he was underneath me and I kissed his mouth and rode back and forth, I felt as if I was in love, and that feeling was all that counted.

My second husband did not want me to be on top. He made sounds, squirming and uncomfortable, when I was on top. He told me a year after we'd gotten together that my body crushed his. His body was smaller than my body. One afternoon, in bed, he nonchalantly told me that I needed to lose a hundred pounds. To shrink myself for him. (Conceivably) to be his equal. I would marry him, cry for years, and leave him, before I realized he did this because he could never make himself big enough—intellectually, financially, sexually—to be *my* equal.

My father stopped letting me sit on his lap when I gained weight. He said he would let me sit on his lap if I lost weight. He said he would buy me a house if I lost weight. He said he would give me ten thousand dollars if I lost weight. When I announced to my parents that I was getting married to my second husband, they responded coldly. My father asked me if I wanted to know why. I told him I didn't. He said, I was hoping you would lose some weight—not much, only a hundred pounds—before you got married.

•

During the last few years of my second marriage, we—
then-husband and I—had sex once annually. I often felt as
if I was begging for sexual attention, because sometimes, I
literally was. I'm a fat woman, a size 22, and sometimes, I'd
forget, even when strangers complimented me on the street
or friends told me I was beautiful, that I was allowed to be a
sexual being. Or that other people might be interested in me
sexually. When I left my second husband, I began having sex
exclusively with younger men.

M was the second younger man I'd connected with online and had sex with. He was Armenian and had loads of
black hair, eyes that almost passed for purple, and a strong,
six-foot frame. I was thirty-seven. He was twenty-seven. I
fell for him the day we cooked a curry together and ate it on
my bedroom floor, naked. He talked to me about his visual
art and hugged his knees and said that he deeply wanted to
make an expression of himself in his work.

•

I spent my late teens dating men in their twenties; my twenties dating men in their thirties; and my thirties married to
a man in his forties. Now, I was reversing the trend.

In 2015, the year before my road trip, I was at a writers'
residency in Marfa. We were not supposed to have visitors,
but they gave us a car. I drove the car two and a half hours

to the El Paso airport to pick M up four weeks into my residency.

M often wore the same outfit: jeans, size 13 shoes, and a plaid shirt. He was wearing these coming down the escalator at Arrivals.

I wore a dress he loved: fitted around the breasts, with a small heart-print over a white background. As I waited for him to get to the ground floor, I could sense a few women staring at me. I could never tell if this was in my imagination, but as a fat woman who enjoys dressing up, I sometimes feel judged, especially at airports, where men and women know they can stare with impunity since they'll never see you again. When M reached the ground floor, we kissed. As we walked toward the exit, I told him that some women had been staring at me. "They probably love your outfit," he said. "Because I love it. Or maybe they're jealous of your tits." The thought of another woman being jealous of my body was alien to me. Why would a slim woman envy me? In a year, I'd know: because I was confident and gorgeous in my rejection of mainstream beauty standards.

On the drive home, he held my hand, something he'd never done before. We reached a deserted seventy-mile stretch of interstate, and I told him to cover his lower half with the sheet I'd packed. This was something we'd both fantasized about. He wiggled out of his jeans and underwear and covered up under the sheet. I took out a big bottle of lube, our favorite brand, and squeezed half a cup all over his dick. Then, I massaged him for half an hour while I drove.

M's penis was perplexingly in a near-constant state of arousal. He orgasmed with difficulty and said he enjoyed that I was not orgasm-centered in my pleasure. He was right. I would get more excited and pleased pleasuring someone for hours than I would having penetrative sex for twenty minutes. I once told a friend what we did, and how much I enjoyed it better than other hookups. "He spends hours touching me," I'd said.

She'd responded, "Don't you get bored?" I often forgot that not everyone enjoyed hours and hours of sex.

I stroked him in the car until we were five miles away from the Texas border patrol checkpoint. I told him to get dressed again, and he pulled up his jeans and we both laughed uncontrollably. When the border patrol officers asked us if we were both citizens, we said yes, and, as I sped away, M took his pants off again.

Twenty miles outside of town, I asked him if he wanted to see the Prada installation, a fake storefront that was created by artists Elmgreen & Dragset ten years earlier. He said he did, pulled his pants back on, and we stopped and parked by three other cars. We circled around the installation, a white cube with shoes and bags behind bulletproof glass, both of us discussing how strange and fun it was, and a man in cargo shorts laughed and told us the installation sucked. We kissed at the back of the building and, behind us, the sun was dipping orange and the desert looked aflame. There were hundreds of dead bugs in all the floodlights attached to the building above us.

In Marfa, M and I stripped off all our clothes and had sex on the couch and on the floor and in the bed. He was the first man in years who'd encouraged me to be on top. He asked me to smother him. He said he loved that all he felt when I was on top were my breasts and my flesh and my cervix. When he said "smother," I heard *mother*.

The West Texas house was warm, and I was worried about falling asleep next to him. We held each other for a few minutes, and then he pulled away, said it was too hot to be so close. I went outside and sat on the porch and worried. How would the next four days go? And would we continue to have fun?

I often wondered why I'd stayed with my second husband so long, when he showed no attraction toward me, unless he was drunk. It's painful to admit to myself, but for those years, I didn't think I was attractive. I knew, objectively, that I had to be, because I often felt good in my skin and wore bright colors and loved my bounce. But, privately, I wondered if I was beautiful in that zoo-attraction way; I felt dehumanized, wondered why a person would choose to be with me when they could be with a woman whose belly didn't flap over her pubic bone, whose back was flat and smooth. I always thought I could either have a kind partner who wasn't attracted to me or a booty-call partner who only wanted to have sex with me. I sometimes had dreams where I was thin. I'd look through clothes in thrift stores and wish I could wear them. When I found something there that fit, it was always costume-y, which just reinforced the idea that I was a circus oddity. It makes me feel so raw to admit it, but sometimes, still, I just don't think I'm loveable or fully human.

In the middle of the night, that first Texas night, M woke me up to kiss me—long, wet kisses—and suckled on my breasts. He pulled me on top of him, and then we fell asleep again, our arms tangled. In the morning, we had sex again, then made poached eggs—I showed him how. He played video games on his phone while I worked in the house's office, which faced a row of wooden shutters and a tangled lawn of stipa leaves.

In the afternoon, we went to look at a rare exhibition of Andy Warhol's *Last Supper* paintings, which were floor-to-ceiling large and imposing. M talked about how much he liked the details at the table, certain saints' faces. We walked around the town hand in hand and took photos of an installation of a car suspended on the nose of its hood.

Watching M wash his dick, tugging at it with each hand, I was flooded with the feeling I got every time I hooked up with a conventionally handsome man. Why was he with me? And did this mean I was beautiful? I hated asking myself these questions. Of course I was beautiful. The men were usually in poly relationships, or much older, but they were always unavailable. With the unavailable ones, I was able to remind myself that I could not keep them, that I was not beautiful enough to keep anyone. M was my first available Hot Guy. What story would I tell myself about him?

That night, I took him out to see the Lights, an atmospheric phenomenon on the desert's horizon, where small orange balls of light bounce and brighten, then fall away. We drove a few miles out of town on a road that led to Mexico, parked in the grass, and stood at a fence and held hands. The stars above us were twinkling, and Venus and Jupiter were orbiting a fraction of a degree from each other. The lights began popping on the horizon, full and then smaller, bouncing left and right. M was afraid of them at first, but I had seen them many times and found them comforting. Eventually, he enjoyed them, too. We stood there for half an hour, kissing and staring at the horizon. That night, we slept in a human pretzel, all our limbs wrapped around the other.

We drove out to a pool, jumped in the water and swam along its almost two acres, fish nibbling at us from time to time. We had a picnic, made tiny salami sandwiches on crackers. It was like being a tween again, swimming and snacking and being goofy. When we got home, M gave me a medical "exam," which he'd scheduled with me a couple of days earlier. "You've given a lot of the medical doctors at our facility bad reviews on Yelp," he said, holding an invisible clipboard. "Now, my methods are unorthodox, but they do get results." I suppressed laughter the entire time he checked my breasts for lumps. When he began using his mouth, I said, feigning shock, "Doctor! Why would you need to use your mouth?" And he said, "The nipple is the lumpiest part of the breast. And the tongue is much more sensitive than hands." Our role-play was always heavy on the play. That afternoon, M, in his doctor guise, practically made me levitate with pleasure.

When, on the fifth day, at a bar with a teepee and a school

bus and a rickety balcony, M told me I was the best lover he'd ever had, and I told him that he was, too, we wondered if it was the openness each of us had for the other; the fact that I was experienced and he was quick to learn; or, maybe, the fact that this would lead nowhere. That last one was implicit.

On his last night in Texas, we went out to see the lights again, but the windshield was thick with bugs, and the sky was cloudy. We parked in the grass, but within minutes, our legs were bitten by mosquitoes and fleas. We held hands and searched on the horizon anyway, intent to duplicate our last meeting, but we saw nothing, and insects began buzzing in our faces, which made M slap at his ears. We ran into the car when we'd had enough, and we laughed all the way back down the road, when a jackrabbit darted out in front of our car and I swerved and screamed, and then he screamed, and then we both were screaming and laughing and losing our breath.

Two weeks later, I would be back home and we would have sex in my bed, but he would leave to go home. He left again. And again. When I confronted him, saying that I thought we'd made a deeper connection in Texas, he responded that he was content the way things were, that he and I were fuck buddies, nothing more. At the end of everything, he was actually an unavailable, attractive twenty-seven-year-old. And I was a beautiful fat woman, making concessions and compromises for a fleeting good time with a handsome man, and a good story. Before he moved out to Seattle for good, M asked me to sit on his lap, and I did, and after asking him three different times if I was hurting him, and after he assured me all three times that I was not, I fully let go, my feet lifting off the carpeted floor, my entire body resting against his.

•

A year later, I was back in Texas. Loneliness. Aimlessness. Large-scale land art and installations felt more like military and border parade floats. I left a week earlier than planned and drove northeast. An hour later, I passed a bar called I DON'T CARE BAR & GRILL.

In Wichita Falls, I met a woman at a Whataburger. She befriended me and we talked about being mothers. She asked me, sheepishly, if she could show me pictures of the son she'd birthed three months earlier, the son who was so premature he died. I could not say no to her; she wanted to unburden her grief for just a few minutes, and I was free to hold it for her. So she pulled up the photo on her phone and slid it to me, and I held the phone and looked at the image, bracing myself for shock. I had never seen a photo of a dead baby outside of war. Her baby was tiny and perfect, and she looked like any new mother in her hospital gown and hair cap. I wished photos like these were more socially acceptable to share, and I told her so. "He was stolen from me," she told me. "Have you ever felt completely robbed?" I told her I had, and when she asked me of what, I told her it was too complicated to explain.

12

THEFT

An ex-student sent me a message, saying that she was going to Ramallah the following month. She asked, Do you want me to bring you anything from the homeland?

The homeland, I said. Bring me the whole homeland.

I wish, she responded.

That wound, that sense of constant ache for home. That feeling that refugees have, that they were robbed of a resting place; it never stops.

Inventory. A key chain; lipsticks, usually the cheap drug-store kind; hair products such as serum at fifteen dollars an ounce; clothes, skirts and tops and dresses; shoes, with my old ones left on the display shelf; a phone line, I used D's social security number to start it, ran a four-hundred-dollar bill before it was shut down; food, all sorts of meals from

Whole Foods, and sundry items from self-serve bulk sections of grocery stores around the country—cashews, tea, dried fruit, crystallized ginger, all of which I labeled as a similar colored product that cost 800 percent less; toilet paper, from bars and libraries and once, The Cheesecake Factory; cocktail glasses, usually still with cocktails in them; ibuprofen; lighters, mostly not on purpose; a very large bag, which I took off a mannequin, slung around my shoulder, shopped the store for an hour while wearing, then walked out with, the plastic security tag making not a sound—I like to think the bag grew accustomed to me; several blocks of printing paper; pens and pencils from offices and people; a compact mirror from the Louvre gift shop.

I am a thief.

Unlike most people, I never stole as a child. I knew it was wrong, and I was afraid of the consequences. It was important for me to be, and to be seen as, a Good Girl. Positive attention shone my direction when I received straight As, when I spoke politely, and when I followed rules.

And then the Gulf War happened. The expulsion of Palestinians, an already-expelled group, from Kuwait happened. Our family moving to Connecticut happened.

•

It was in Connecticut that I stole my very first thing. I had a job on the main avenue. The job was at an independent bodycare shop, where I shrink-wrapped lotions for elderly women.

The avenue was a long, multi-block shopping street, lined, top to bottom, with pricey restaurants and high-end clothing stores. After work, I walked across the street to smoke a secret cigarette. I was fifteen years old. Boys at school called me Tits, and girls called me Rhoda. After my cigarette, I would walk into a gift shop. There were toys and buttons and pens and mugs and key chains with "American" names on them. None of the key chains had my name. Nothing in all of the world had my name. This meant I did not exist. Which then meant that I was invisible. Which lead me to believe I could take whatever I wanted. So I took a blank keychain, and I walked out. Nothing happened. No alarm sounded. I was thrilled and warm all over, until I realized I had no keys, no place of my own, and that the keychain was useless to me.

My mother sometimes picked me up from work. My mother did not work. She got married so she wouldn't have to work. That is what she wanted, what she believed. My mother would stay in her car outside and wait for me. At the end of each shift, I would sweep the floors of the shop, blaring PJ Harvey and Prince and Björk over the din of the heavy rain outside. When the floors were clean, I'd lock up the inventory room and the doors to the shop, and I'd run from the shop to my mother's car (the car we all used, because we could only afford one), dodging the rain, and as soon as I would get in her car, my mother would chastise me. She'd say, don't you dare sweep for them again. Do you hear me? I never want to see you sweeping floors.

But it's part of my job, I would say, and I don't mind it at all. It's kind of . . . (the word I was looking for was *medita-tive*, but at fifteen, I didn't know it yet).

If I see you sweeping again, you quit that job, she'd say. Because to my mother, work was humiliation.

I got a paycheck every two weeks. I spent my money on whatever I wanted: usually books, clothes, cigarettes, and weed. But after a few months, I didn't like working. My mother was right, I decided. Labor was such a scam.

And I stole.

In college, my parents put me on a cold-lunch plan. I stole dinner from the dining hall, pretending I was just there to study. I stole a billiard ball from the campus poolroom when a woman told me I wasn't really Arab, just a descendent of white people who once lived in Arab countries. I stole flowers from wealthy neighborhood gardens when not a single person at my college, male or female, wanted to spend any sexy time with me.

Plus the time I suspected I was pregnant: I stole a pack of pregnancy tests from CVS.

•

Years later, I will tell my son this story. I will tell him that I discovered that he existed on a stolen pregnancy test. He will be getting ready to move out of our house. He will laugh and tell me he loves me. I wonder how I thought I could raise a child alone when I couldn't afford a pregnancy test. And yet, my son says that he never knew we were poor.

I hate menstruation. And the fact that I have to pay money every four weeks so that I won't bleed on my office chair infuriates me. So does the price of tampons.

My favorite heist: I was at a Target. I was menstruating. I placed two large packs of tampons in the basket part of my shopping cart. I paid for my cat food, the cleaning products. I did not pay for the tampons, which were still in the basket, under my purse. When I pushed my cart toward the door, I realized that I had to pee, but I didn't know where to keep my cart with all my purchases in it. I saw a security guard and the idea thrilled me. No! I wouldn't do that. I shouldn't do that. I did that. I pushed my cart to him, asked him to watch my things while I used the bathroom, and he agreed. In the toilet stall, when I wiped after I peed, I noticed that my vulva was wet from excitement. I walked out of the bathroom and a pulse of pleasure radiated between my legs when I saw the security guard keeping watch over my stolen tampons, the ones I'd be pushing into my pussy every day for the next four days.

•

I love heist films. I think about robbing banks regularly. I read about famous thieves with ardor and envy and ambition. My favorites are Parisienne drag queens who sashayed into a diamond store and put everyone there in a corner, like naughty dunces, and then just cracked the display glass and took everything and were never caught. Goddesses.

•

I am at a party with wealthy white people who think they are not wealthy. I ask them if they want to do an art heist. They tell me that Donald Judd's pieces are worth millions. I say I have seen one cop the entire time I've been here, and that we could get away with it. I'm joking, of course, but am I? A handsome guy tells me there are three police officers here and they are not to be fucked with. He says they pull him over twice a week. He's white, so he is still alive. Everyone wants nothing to do with the heist conversation.

•

D. B. Cooper was never my jam. It's romantic, I guess, in a straight-white-guy kind of way. Instead of D. B. Cooper's story, I have always been electrified by Leila Khaled's. Khaled hijacked a plane in the seventies to bring attention to the Palestinian cause. No one was hurt. But sometimes I imagine that she jumped off the plane and took Palestine with her, and got away with it.

•

I read about kleptomaniacs. I discover that each of them steals because something irreplaceable was stolen from them. That something was taken from them, and they will never forget.

•

I think of my baby vagina bleeding, of how many times I've been evicted from homes. I think about wars. And I think of the original wound. I think about how I can never tell anyone what my hometown is, because I don't have a hometown. I think about how I'm not from anywhere. I think about history.

And I distill my thoughts and focus on that wound. That first loss. I think about Palestine. I think about acres of land being stolen, trees uprooted. I think about the fact of my Palestinian-ness, my name and my grandmother's name in the big computer at Tel Aviv airport, the record of my existence, because of which, ironically, I cannot return. I think about people who left their homes, packing for two weeks, because they thought they would come back. I think about how many times I have done that, too.

•

The last time I stole was about a month ago. I walked out of a pharmacy holding two bottles of vitamins. I don't always go through with it. Sometimes I place an item in my bag and think about walking away with it. And at the very last moment, I take it out of my dark bag and into the light, and place it on the register's conveyor belt.

13

MONUMENT

From Texas, I drove on to Oklahoma City and checked into an old hotel. In my white-walled cavernous hotel room, I heard the news about Alton Sterling, a Black man shot point-blank in the head by police. I watched the video knowing that it would make me rageful.

White men with money sat across the hotel lobby from me in red velvet chairs and sofas, under a painting of white men sitting on sofas. The real white men talked about Donald Trump, and the longer I looked at them, the longer their bodies seemed to be surrounded with red blood.

My hotel was built in the 1800s by enslaved Black people. Now a white bartender was complaining to another bartender, a woman, who had to emotionally massage his pain: he said he'd been captured on film by a news crew and that they'd asked his permission to use his likeness and he'd said yes. But when he watched the news that night he'd been cut out of the segment.

He was very upset telling the other bartender about this.

I thought I was going to be on the news, he said, but they cut me out.

I got cut out of the news.

They cut me.

Out of the news.

Alton Sterling dying, being murdered, every minute on the news. Over and over again. Palestinian children in white burial cloth. Black and brown bodies wishing they weren't on the news. Mothers wishing they didn't live in an empire or under the thumb of one, an empire that depends on the myth of their resilience.

•

Before breakfast I walked outside the hotel with my dog, and the valet parker wanted to talk to us. He liked my dog. He reached over to pet her, and I noticed a tattoo on his wrist. I asked him if it was a tattoo in Arabic. He said yes and showed it to me. It said *I love*. I told him, "It says, 'I love.'" He said, "It says, 'my love.'" It said *I love*. But I nodded. He said an Iraqi friend wrote it for him. An Iraqi guy, he said. He used to work here. I asked him if he heard of the bombing in Baghdad a few days ago. He nodded, sadly. I said the Global North was fucked-up for living in comfort at the expense of the Global South. He said yes, and we acted like our lives were so hard. He shook his head. I wanted to embrace him.

I drove through Bricktown. There was a Flaming Lips Alley. I drove past bars shut down because it was morning, and the fanciest Sonic I have ever seen—a brick building, no drive-through.

I went north and wound my way to the Alfred P. Murrah Federal Building, to the site of the Oklahoma City bombing of 1995. It was no longer a bombed-out building at all. Years of living in the Middle East, of growing up around sites of trauma and war, made it difficult for me to process memorial sites.

The serenity, cleanliness, sterile slate gray tile, water, life replacing horror.

This site had all of that. It is across the street from a church. There is a small painting of a Jesus who appears biracial, Indigenous and white. He embraces the nineteen children who died in the bombing.

The site was an outdoor memorial, with an artificial and shallow reflective pool where the building once stood. Visitors were encouraged to sit near the field of empty chairs, which were a physical representation of the chairs of the dead. Near this, there was a small section of the original building left. Salvaged granite. It was beautiful. The top of it was devastated, cracked, burned, and bombed. It reached up toward a tree, which was labeled "survivor tree" by the memorial, and up to the sky.

The bombing was the deadliest act of "domestic" terrorism at the time. One hundred and sixty-eight people died; hundreds were injured. The white perpetrators were sentenced to death (Timothy McVeigh) and prison (Terry Nichols). McVeigh was executed three months before 9/11. He remains the only terrorist who received an official execution sentence by U.S. courts.

•

In the shower that morning, I started my period. When I looked down at my feet on the ceramic bathtub, I saw a small blood clot between them, dark brown, a long Y: the shape of the Nile.

•

From Oklahoma City, I drove to St. Louis. As I wound through Missouri, I heard on the radio that there was a city nearby, in the Midwest, whose electricity ran on the skin of women. The city power plant was almost shut down, but strippers in the district kept it on with their donations. When the lights were on at night you could gaze out at the place and understand how women's bodies literally made the city shimmer.

•

In Springfield, every billboard screamed, "This is a country fair." One said, "Visit the Uranus fudge factory." There was a series of Dixie Stampede billboards, and a series of Fantastic Caverns billboards that feature weird Okie people, in strange and obvious costume getups. Basically, people performing whiteness. Then miles of grass. The only representation of a person of color I saw for two hundred miles was a giant Cherokee statue outside a travel center back in Eastern Oklahoma. It felt as if I was in a temporary place, the way a carnival sets up and then leaves. That's what I was getting from this part of America. Outwardly not committed, temporary. There were no homes. I drove past huge trailer-home lots. Nothing was here to stay.

•

Signs along the way:

Leaving Kiowa-Comanche-Apache Reservation

Leaving Sac and Fox Nation

No sign welcoming drivers to the nations and reservations, which I loved. *You are not welcome here. We'll let you know when you're wanted, which is never.*

As I drove I remembered the story inside Leslie Marmon Silko's 1977 classic, *Ceremony*, about a Native man who returns from World War II, and the ways his trauma was healed by Native history and folklore. In one section of the book, a group of Indigenous American witches hold a contest hundreds of years ago about who can cast the best spell or create the best ceremony. And the one that does is the one that calls the white people over, the one that predicts colonizers. It's always been such a hair-raising and terrifying idea, one that places power back in the hands of the oppressed, as if to say to the colonizer, "We sent for you."

I was pulled over by a Missouri police officer for speeding. There was a larger SUV going the same exact speed as I was, but I was the one who got pulled over and my hair was extra frizzy and big this day. The cop approached my car very gingerly—he was slim, pale, and short, and he wore a wide-brim hat. As soon as he saw my face, his body language changed. If I seemed like a light-skinned woman of color from behind, I seemed like a white woman from the front. My dog climbed up on the window frame, and the cop asked if she was friendly. I said she was very friendly. He asked for my license and registration. I reached into my bag. I brought out my wallet. I leaned over and gave him my license. At no point did he seem threatened or pull a gun on me or kill me. I even asked if he could give me a warning. I was going 86 in a 70. I understood my privilege and actually requested a warning. He said I was receiving a citation because 86 was too high for a warning, but his inflection was apologetic. He gave me my ticket, which said I was going 85. I went along my way, alive. In one piece.

•

From my notes the next morning:

Philando Castile was shot dead yesterday in a routine traffic stop. He'd been stopped forty-six times up until that point. He paid off every single citation. The police officer shot him anyway. I walk around Soulard and go to the farmers' market. An elderly man wants me to sit with him to talk about my dog, so I do. On the way into St. Louis there were signs: PASS WITH CARE. My fat Arab body continues to pass for white.

14

INSIDE THE
YELLOW LINE

Just after New Year's of 2005, my younger brother, R, then a senior at the University of Maryland, came home to D.C. after visiting our parents in Kuwait. The security people at Dulles Airport detained and questioned him for hours, then told him he was a deportable alien. He had two weeks to surrender to authorities. Once he did, he was sent to a jail in Virginia.

A few days after his imprisonment, I got an email from his lawyer that said he needed contact lens solution. I rushed out and bought it, sent it off with his prisoner ID number on the envelope, went home, and spent the rest of the day in bed.

Unlike my brother, I was born in the U.S. and never had to work for my little blue passport. My Egyptian/Palestinian family did; they all took tests and held little flags and swore to do or not do things—all but my brother, who was too flaky at eighteen to fill out the proper forms or take buses to the right offices. He was left behind in our family's Becoming American journey. In 2001, he was living with students who sold pot. When they got busted, he went to jail for five days and did a few dozen hours of community service. And he was being deported four years later because that had been "a crime of moral turpitude."

My brother called me collect, and I got up the courage to ask him what the jail in Virginia looked like.

"They let us congregate for religious reasons inside a small strip. They seal it off with yellow tape. You can pray or talk inside the yellow line."

A few days later, my father called me in a panic.

"Your brother is turning into a fundamentalist," he said.

"Don't be ridiculous."

"He told mom he is writing a sermon for this Friday's prayers."

I pictured my brother reading a sermon in the small space, his hand resting on the yellow tape on the floor.

"That's so sweet," I said.

"It is not sweet; it is crazy. Please stop him. He will come out of that jail a fanatic!"

"That'll never happen," I said. "Don't you know him at all? He is just finding a way to cope." I couldn't tell my father that my brother liked liquor and women too much to become religious.

•

In order to get the government to reverse the deportation, we hired a psychologist to determine the level of hardship my brother's absence would cause us. By the time the therapist called me, the lawyer had written me an email saying I was the only sane person in my family.

His final court date was March 22. I met my parents in a hotel in the same building as the courthouse. At dinner the night before the hearing, my father couldn't figure out how to work the pepper shaker, because he always thinks things are much harder than they actually are.

After dinner, we took the elevator up to our rooms. "I'm sick," my father said. "The therapist gave me my file today. I need help."

I'd been waiting to hear those words all my life.

My mother, who has always hated therapists because she thinks all people talk about in therapy is what a terrible person she is, interrupted. "I passed the test. The doctor said I was severely depressed. I wanted him to think so! I wanted to prove the hardship!" She smiled and danced around the hotel room.

The morning of the hearing, we all sat in the waiting area with other families. The rows of white plastic chairs faced a wall. It felt like we were all on a plane, being deported. Inside the courtroom, my brother was on a monitor, defending his moral fiber. An hour passed. "Maybe the judge will just let him out after this," I said.

"That is wishful thinking," my father said, closing his eyes. Everything had to be like that pepper shaker.

Less than fifteen minutes later, the judge stopped the hearing. "I've heard enough," he said, leafing through dozens of family photos.

He released my brother and reversed the deportation order.

•

But it wasn't over. I had to map the jail, print out the directions, and sit in the car with my parents as they screamed at each other all the way from D.C., through traffic, across Virginia.

Four hours after we set out, we reached the jail. We parked outside the entrance and waited. My brother's silhouette appeared against the electric fence. Soon we were embracing him. His hair was shaved close. In the car, he told us stories of the men he'd been living with.

As we approached College Park, my father grew impatient with the printed map and the unfamiliar roads. He ignored my brother's directions, and soon, we were going the wrong way on a one-way road. After all we'd done, my father jeopardized our lives out of impatience. Or maybe he was determined that he wouldn't let the government do the destruction for him. In any case, by the time we reached my brother's apartment, we were all anxious to leave the small prison of the rental car. We stood awkwardly around Raed's coffee table, reluctant to admit that we got along a lot easier in crisis. A few minutes passed, and we shuffled our feet and said goodbye. My brother waved to us from the doorway, as though we'd just spent the last few hours visiting, and were now heading home.

•

When my brother was four, he broke into a parked Cadillac in our apartment building's parking lot. He and his best friend hung out in the big American car's velvety seats and pretended to drive, their short legs dangling high above the floor. A neighbor saw them and brought my brother home. My father yelled all that night. Then he stood up, knowing what he had to do. He would take my brother to the police; he would put him in jail. To teach him a lesson. He would.

"Get ready," he told my brother.

I watched as my brother went to the front door, bent down, and silently, without the smallest murmur of resistance, strapped on his small leather shoes.

Then he straightened up, looked down the hallway, and waited.

15

BOATERS

For a very long time, I intensely disliked the word *naturalized*. It made me feel as if my family's very existence was unnatural, and would only change once they became citizens. I looked up the word to avail myself of this feeling, and I enjoyed the biological definition—that to naturalize a plant was to make sure it could live wild in a land where it was not indigenous. The *wild* part was the part I adored. We were living wild in America. Until we were not.

●

In April of 2013, I was still in my sexless marriage when the Boston-bomber manhunt began. The image that later surfaced, of the eight-year-old who died, holding a sign that says *no more hurting people*, is seared indelibly on my memory.

•

"He looks like your son," my ex said, when they released a photo of the younger Boston bomber. I looked at the photo. My son is darker skinned, but yes, there is a slight resemblance. The eyes, for one. The nose, too.

•

Walking with the Palestinian poet S once through Jersey City, we talked about our historical and present uprootings. She was being kicked out of her apartment after over a decade and a half of living there. In her kitchen, she pointed out of her windows at where the towers used to be. She had seen them burn from where we stood. I have recurring dreams that I will be forced to move from my house. Just last night, I dreamt that people came for me, that I didn't have time to pack, that I moved to a room with flooded sewage. My mother showed up in the dream in one of her nylon nighties and helped me clean up.

•

I am an American, Chicago-born. Just like Bellow said. I left with my family six weeks after my birth, and we returned thirteen years later. My brother, until a few weeks before Trump's election, was still a Jordanian citizen—because he could not be a citizen of Palestine, since there is no such state—and a legal U.S. resident. My parents had left my brother and me behind a few years after our immigration and gone back to the Middle East. My entire family is awful with paperwork, so much so that my brother never filed the paperwork he was supposed to file or showed up to the places he was supposed to show up when it was time for him to become a citizen. Consequently, he and I were, until recently, the only ones in our family who were not naturalized.

●

S said that all of us children of immigrants are terrible with paperwork. I told S that our friend L, who died of breast cancer a few years ago, was good with paperwork. I clarified that L told me she had become better with paperwork after she survived the first bout of cancer. "That's why she made peace with paperwork," S says. "She knew she was going to die."

●

"But Boston isn't a war zone," I heard people say in the days of the manhunt, when they were asked to have empathy with Syrians, Palestinians, victims of drone strikes. "Have you been to Boston?" my friend J responded to them. "Every corner of that place is historically a war zone."

•

I was filing back taxes and looking through my old receipts. I'd moved to Texas briefly before moving to California ten years ago, and I used Mayflower to move. That was the only time anyone in my family had anything to do with anything named Mayflower. We didn't move to America on the Mayflower; we moved to America on EgyptAir.

•

The last time I took my son to Egypt, he was only eight. I left him for two nights with my mother and went to Cairo to hang out with some writers. One of those writers, a graphic novelist, was arrested last week during a protest. I found out on my Twitter feed in between updates about the Boston bombing. He was my driver during those two days in Cairo, and we commiserated over our children's other parents, over the awfulness of divorce. I became angry with him later, at a coffee shop, when I'd taken my hair out of a ponytail and he'd said that my hair looked better down. I was hot, I'd shouted at him, and you don't know me. He was released on bail during the days of the manhunt.

•

In 1999, a pilot of an EgyptAir flight let go of the controls and left God to be pilot.

But since God doesn't know how to fly a 767, everyone on board perished. I was living in Texas, in a family housing unit with my son, then three years old. We were hanging out on the playground with dozens of friends, all of us from different backgrounds. It was the America I had always thought I would live in. When she found out about the flight, a fellow mother, a Latina from a border town, said, "God, those people who cover their heads." I had stopped sleeping with a man the previous week because he'd said that this woman and her husband were having babies young because they were from Brownsville, a Texas border town.

•

In August of 2001, I moved with my son into a trailer on a little piece of property in a small Texas town outside of Austin. On 9/11, our white landlord came by and strung up a giant American flag. "This is for your protection," he said, because I'd told some neighbors I was Arab American. Those first nights, I made my son, then almost five, sleep in my room, not in his, which was closer to the main road.

•

The week after the Boston bombing, my son dreamed that he was in a classroom full of people, and his chemistry teacher asked all the Black, Latino, Asian, and white students to stand off to one side, and everyone else to stand to the other.

•

After hanging out with Egyptian writers for two days, my mother brought my son out to Cairo from Alexandria on the train, and we all went to dinner near the Nile. My son and I took a ride in a small canoe after the sun set, a man rowing us through the water. My son asked me if he could leave a wish in the water. I gave him a piece of paper and he scrawled *happiness for everyone*, folded the piece of paper, and released it in the river.

•

"Boaters," I've heard young Arab Americans call their immigrant parents and their parents' friends in Dearborn,

Michigan. "Ten years in America," the younger Boston bomber had once tweeted, "I want out."

When they finally found the bomber, out of all the places he could have hidden in Boston, he was curled up inside a boat.

16

IMAGINING MYSELF IN PALESTINE

When my sister got a job in Ramallah in 2011, teaching music to children, I knew I would want to visit her. I had not been to Palestine since 1993. I had planned to go back in the summer of 1996, but I was pregnant and unmarried. My parents did not want to speak to me, let alone take me with them, in such a shameful condition, to the West Bank. I never went back with family after that. I led my own life. I moved about a dozen times over the following fifteen years—an American nomad. I didn't want to visit the West Bank and be at the mercy of family. If I ever visited, I would do so independently. When my sister moved to Ramallah she found an apartment of her own, and it had an extra room. It was the perfect time to go. My husband booked my flight, and, thrilled, I told my sister I was coming.

But trouble began weeks before I boarded my flight to Tel Aviv's Ben Gurion Airport. I had heard horror stories about a detention area there, dubbed the Arab Room, and in my anxious and neurotic style, I had emailed a dozen people—American academics and artists of Arab, Indian, Jewish, and European descent—and asked them what I was supposed to tell the immigration officers at Ben Gurion once I arrived. They all wanted to know if I was using my American passport, and I assured them that I was. The vast majority told me not to tell the officers I would be staying at my sister's in Ramallah. They said this would cause trouble, and they offered up the names of friends and family for my use. The generosity of people poured in, and I was advised to say that I was staying with this writer, or that visual artist, or this former IDF soldier—people I had never met, but who had volunteered themselves to be my proxy hosts. A friend of mine, who is a phenomenal photojournalist, gave me her phone number and said to tell the officers I would be staying with her, and I agreed. She told me to prepare for the officers to call her themselves once I gave them her number, as this is something they are known to do.

•

I'd been so afraid of facing the guards at the airport that I had a difficult time imagining the rest of my trip. I would try to picture myself walking around Ramallah with my sister, or attending a concert, or visiting my aunts, or seeing the separation wall, or staying at the American Colony Hotel for an evening, and I would draw a blank. There was a wall there, too, between my thoughts and Palestine.

•

Growing up, my Palestinian identity was mostly tied to my father. He was the Palestinian in the family, and when we went back to the West Bank it was to see his brothers and sisters and parents. We always entered Palestine through Amman, crossing the Allenby Bridge over the River Jordan and waiting in endless inspection lines. I remember these trips dragging on through morning and midday and well into the afternoon. My father would sit quietly, and when I complained, my Egyptian mother would tell me that the Israelis made it difficult for us to cross into the West Bank. She told me that they wanted us to give up, that they would prefer we never go back. "We must not let them win," she'd said. My relationship with my Palestinian identity was cemented when I enrolled in a PLO-sponsored girls' camp as a tween. We learned nationalistic songs and dances and created visual art that reflected our understanding of the occupation. After my family and I moved to America in 1991, my Palestinian identity shifted again, and I began to see myself as an Arab American. My father's fiery rants on Palestine died out when Yitzhak Rabin was murdered by a Jewish Israeli extremist. I remember my father weeping in our American wood-paneled den. He said that Rabin had been the Palestinians' last chance.

There weren't, as far as I could see, any other Arabs boarding US Airways flight 796 to Tel Aviv. On the airplane, I found myself surrounded by Christian missionaries and Evangelicals and observant Jewish men. The group across the aisle had their Bibles out, the man sitting next to me read from a miniature Torah, and as the flight took off, I found myself reciting a verse from the Quran, almost against my will. All the praying was contagious.

I spoke to no one on the plane, and no one spoke to me.

As we descended into Israel, the blue Mediterranean floated by below us. We saw the shore of Tel Aviv, and the buildings along it. An American teenager sitting in front of me started shouting, "It's so pretty! It's so pretty!" She wouldn't have any trouble clearing passport control, I was sure.

When we landed, everyone on the plane clapped, something I thought only Lebanese people did, and I smiled. I turned on my phone and called my sister and let her know I had arrived, and that I would call her on the other side of customs and immigration. I was only an hour away from her. I took a deep breath and did something superstitious, as I tend to do when I am feeling powerless and anxious. I flipped to a random page in my passport, hoping to find meaning and reassurance in it. On the page I flipped to was a picture of an old steamship, presumably in the shadow of

Ellis Island. I found the image inspiring, calming, and I felt ready to face customs.

I had deleted anything on my personal website critical of Israel, which amounted to about 160 posts. I had deleted the section in my Wikipedia entry that said that I was a Palestinian writer. It had been unsettling, deleting my Palestinianness in order to go back to Palestine. I had been told that the Israeli officers might confiscate my phone and read my Facebook posts and Twitter feed, so I temporarily deactivated my Facebook account and locked my tweets. The entire endeavor left me feeling erased.

I had read an article about the hundreds of activists that had flown into Ben Gurion Airport in July of 2011. They had all been detained over the weekend and then flown back to their countries of origin. Only one of them had made it through. When she was asked how she managed it, she said that she chose the "smiliest" immigration officer and stood in her line. So, when I entered the immigration hall, I did the same. The agent I chose was blonde and young, and her line was moving the fastest. I stood, waited, and tried to relax.

There was only one person in the line in front of me, but the woman officer went to the back of her booth and a young bearded man took her place. He did not seem "smiley" at all. I considered switching lanes, but I knew I would look suspicious. So I waited.

When it was my turn, I gave the officer my blue American passport. As he scanned it, I noticed that he had unbelievably long lashes. He thumbed through the pages, and I was afraid of what he would make of the Lebanese stamp. He asked me what my purpose was for visiting Israel. I told him it was my spring break and I had come to visit friends. He asked me where I was staying. I did as I'd been told and said I was staying in Jerusalem, with the photojournalist. He picked up a black telephone. When he hung up, he told me to go wait in the room in the corner. I asked him if I could have my passport back, and he said no. I asked him when I would be getting my passport back, and he didn't answer. He only repeated that I needed to go to the room in the corner.

I crossed the immigration hall diagonally and entered the Arab Room. Sitting in the room and waiting were a young Arab man and an older Arab woman in hijab; two Black men in African garb, one of whom was holding an iPad; two middle-aged Arab women in hijab; one dark-haired Tunisian American woman in a long skirt; one woman in a Whitney Houston T-shirt, her hair gathered up in a turban; and one dark-skinned Arab woman in a pantsuit. It was readily transparent that we had all been racially profiled. A young man joined us and got on his phone. I heard him saying, "No, they just finished questioning me. I'm half-Egyptian. I should be out soon." I got up and told the woman guard at the door that I needed to go to the bathroom, and she nodded. When I came back to the room, I sat down and took out a magazine, reading as calmly as I could. About twenty minutes passed before a redhead, who couldn't have been older than nineteen, summoned me down the hallway. I followed him to an office where a few brown men were answering questions. The redhead asked me to take a seat and swiped my passport through at his station.

He asked me, "What is the name of your father? And what is the name of your father's father?"

My father and I at that point hadn't spoken in four years. We would not speak for another three.

I gave the redhead the names he'd asked. He noted something on a piece of paper and asked me where my father was from. My father was born in 1950, when the West Bank was part of Jordan, so I told the redhead that my father was a Jordanian American.

"So, he is from Jordania?" the redhead said, pronouncing the word *Jordan* wrong. I had no idea how someone could mispronounce a place they shared a border with, but Israel often strikes me as a place that doesn't want to believe where it actually is on the map.

I said that technically, yes, he was. "Where was he born?" he said, and, cornered, I told the redhead that my father had been born in Jenin. He noted something else on a piece of paper, gave it to a man who seemed like a superior, and asked me to go to another room in an opposite corner. When I said that I was a writer and an American citizen, born in Chicago, he shrugged and instructed me, again, to go to the room in the opposite corner.

I went to the room, and I waited.

My father had said in an email that, by writing about sex in my novel so shamelessly, I had disregarded the legacy of my Palestinian family, which, he claimed, had defeated Napoleon.

I always thought he was being dramatic about Napoleon, but eventually I looked it up. In a book titled *Rediscovering Palestine: Merchants and Peasants in Jabal Nablus 1700–1900*, I found the Jarrar family, and I found Napoleon. The emperor's attempt to conquer Palestine had been stopped short in 1799, and an ancestor of mine named Shaykh Yousef Jarrar, the mayor of Jenin, had written a poem "in which he exhorted his fellow leaders . . . to unite under one banner against the French forces." I'd never heard of this poet-warrior ancestor before, but I had given my son the middle name Yousef, as if by instinct.

A woman wearing seven rings on her fingers, and a lot of blue eye makeup caked around her eyes, emerged from a small interrogation room and asked me to join her. She told me to close the door behind me. The room was the size of a walk-in closet, and I knew it had been built to intimidate travelers. The woman said she liked my necklace, and we spoke about jewelry for a few minutes. I admired one of her rings in particular, and she smiled and said it was from Egypt. She then swiped my passport and asked me about my parents' names, again. This time, I told her I was not in communication with my father, and that I was an American citizen, and a writer. She did not seem to care about this information one way or the other, and she spoke my grandmother's name. I hadn't heard my grandmother's name in years. She had died in the early eighties. I told the officer this, and she nodded, and she gave me the names of many of my ancestors. I wanted to ask her for her grandmother's name, but I gave her the name of my friend in Jerusalem and my Israeli publisher in Or Yehuda instead.

"Your publisher?" she said, confused, and I said, yes, my book had been translated into Hebrew and published in Israel. I could see her computer screen. She plugged in my publisher's name and my friend's, in Hebrew, and their addresses came up. The program she was using looked clunky and old, but it held information on every citizen in Israel. At this point, things began to feel Kafkaesque.

She said that there was a Palestinian ID attached to my name. I told her I had no such ID. She said that I had entered the West Bank with the ID in 1993, and that they had record of the entry. She said that this would be a problem. When I tried to plead my case, she asked me to put my right finger on a glowing red scanner. Then my left finger. She took my photograph and asked me to go back to the first waiting room. When I asked her what I should expect, she said she wasn't sure.

Half an hour later, a group of teenage guards took me to baggage claim. I asked them if I could speak to someone from the American embassy, or the consulate, and they nodded, smirking. A few minutes later, I asked them what we were doing there, and they said we needed to find my bag. I said that my carry-on bag was my only bag, and they seemed shocked. I travel a lot, I told them, which they seemed to find suspicious. They asked me why, and I said I was a writer. They frowned at me. We waited for more guards. It must have been their shift change. The baggage claim was deserted. In the corner, a few guards were giving each other massages. The guards I was waiting with gave each other high fives and chatted about teenage stuff. I kept asking what we were waiting for, and they ignored me.

Finally, they took me to a room in the corner of the baggage-claim area. It was becoming clear to me that at Ben Gurion, unjust things happened in corners. The guards asked me to open my bags. I did as I was told. I noted that the room was filthy. The Israelis were concerned with showing a clean and gleaming exterior—the floors of the airport outside shone—but for suspected threats and people like myself, behind closed doors, tucked away in dirty corners, they hadn't bothered. A very butch young woman asked me to follow her. She led me to yet another room, where the walls were faded and filthy, and the floor was covered in dirty carpet, littered with small bits of paper and hair clips. It reeked of intimidation, and of humiliation.

I don't believe in hokey things such as souls or spirits, but I could sense a deeply disturbing feeling in the room. There, though I was not strip-searched, the young guard poked and searched every millimeter of my clothes and underclothes. I tried to keep myself distracted, so I wouldn't weep. I tried to keep my spirits up. I did not want to allow these teenagers to rob me of my dignity.

When I came out of the room, a boy with pimples, who looked like he was my son's age, was going through my clothes. Above him hung a tourist poster for the Dead Sea. The poster read: *The Dead Sea; Where Time Seems to Stand*

Still. I had been in Ben Gurion for over two hours and knew the feeling. It was as if I existed outside of time, suspended in a strange molasses of interrogation.

When he was done checking all my clothes, he asked me if I needed any help repacking the bag. I said that I didn't, and that I had a system for packing. "You have a system?" he shouted. I told him this was an American idiom. Still, he watched me closely as I packed.

I was worn down and angry. The teenagers escorted me back to the waiting room, the Arab Room, where there was now a new guard. A few people were gone, and a few new people had arrived, but it was still an Arab Room.

The woman with all the rings walked in with my passport in her hand and said that she was sorry, but that I was not allowed to enter Israel. She said she had spoken to her supervisor, and that he had decided that I was not to enter. When I asked her if I could speak to him personally, she said she would ask, and she walked away with my passport. I never saw her again, nor did I see the supervisor.

I called my sister and told her the news. She was devastated. A friend of mine had been waiting in his car outside the airport to drive me to her, and I called him, too. When I told him now that I was being shipped back to the U.S., he said, furious, that he would call his friends at the U.S. consulate. When I called him back, he said that there was nothing they could do, and that I was banned by law from entering Israel because I was considered Palestinian.

I told a guard that I was a diabetic, and hungry, and an

hour later someone wordlessly brought me a sandwich. I began to feel like a prisoner, grateful for a dry bit of bread and cheese. Halfway through the sandwich, I asked the other people in the room if they were hungry. A middle-aged woman in hijab said she was, and I gave her the rest of the sandwich. A large guard appeared over me, hovering, and asked me in Arabic where I was from. I answered reflexively in English, "I am from here. And from California." He asked me, in Arabic, where I was going after the airport. I said, in English, that I was going to Jerusalem. He walked away and accused me of pretending not to know Arabic. He said the word *Arabic* hatefully. I followed him and said, in Arabic, "OK, I do speak Arabic. Where do I want to go after this? I want to go to a bar with my friends." He laughed at me and said I could go to a bar when I got back to America.

After a while, I was the last person in the room. It had high stone walls that spanned every floor of the airport, and when I tried to look all the way up, I could not see the ceiling. I felt as if I were trapped in a strange, deep well.

An elderly man who was not Jewish but who had attempted to make aliyah was put in the room with me. When they told him he was being deported back to the U.S., he said he would not leave. The guard said to him, "I could do this the nice way, or I could do this the not-nice way." It was ludicrous in more ways than one, to hear a nineteen-year-old speak to an old man that way.

An hour later, the bearded young man who had originally questioned me at the immigration hall became my guard. When I tried to go to the bathroom, he said I was not allowed. This made me nervous. I had been allowed to go before. I told him so. "Well, it's different now," he said.

"Different how?" I asked. "Am I under detention?"

He would not answer me. I told him that I was an American citizen and that I demanded to know whether or not I was under detention. He closed his eyes, then opened them, and said, reluctantly, "Yes."

I lost it. I demanded to see someone from the embassy or the consulate. He ignored me. I said that he needed to take me to the bathroom. He said no. I lifted up my dress and pretended to squat, and I shouted, "Fine, then I will go to the bathroom right here!"

He became angry and shouted to another guard to take me to the bathroom. When she said she couldn't, he took me himself. He insisted on the gender-neutral handicapped toilet, and he waited outside the stall. When I was done, he checked the stall after me, to make sure that I had not concocted a bomb out of my pubic hair. I laughed at him, and he angrily took me back to the detention room.

I waited two more hours. Whenever a guard came into the room, I would ask him what was going on with my passport, and what I could expect. The guard would look down at me and sneer, "You have to wait. You have to wait." When I told him I had been waiting for hours, he only repeated, "You have to wait." My wait felt interminable. In his speech to the UN, Mahmoud Abbas quoted the late Palestinian poet Mahmoud Darwish's poem "State of Siege." He read,

"Standing here. Sitting here. Always here. / Eternally here, / we have one aim and one aim only: to continue to be." And he added, "And we shall be." The state of sitting, of standing, of waiting, is the principal state of the Palestinian; it is the state of the refugee, of the oppressed, of the outsider, of the writer.

Eventually, two female guards came to tell me what time I would board the flight back to the U.S. When they did, I burst into tears. I had been holding out hope, right to the last. After they left, I was stuck with the male guard again, the one who had picked up the phone in the immigration booth.

I asked him if I could board a flight elsewhere—to Amman, or Cairo, even Paris. I wanted to go somewhere, at least, even if I couldn't see my sister.

"No," he said. "You have to go back from where you came."

I said that this was unacceptable, and that I wanted the choice to go elsewhere.

This time, he shouted it. "No. You must go back from where you came."

"Are you from *The Lord of the Rings*?" I said.

He narrowed his eyes at me and snapped, "Come with me." He made me stand in a hallway for twenty minutes, as punishment. I made fun of his long eyelashes. I asked him if he was related to Snuffleupagus. He ignored me.

An hour or so passed, and a guard came and eventually escorted me to flight 797, back to the U.S. We bypassed security, avoiding a scene, and when we got to the airplane the guard gave my passport to the flight attendant, an American.

"Do not give her back her passport until you arrive in America," he said.

She squinted at him, confused. "What do you mean?"

"This woman was denied entry and must return to the United States. Do not give her this passport until you have left Israel and arrived in America."

She looked at me and nodded, frowning.

I went to my seat, which was in the middle of the middle row, the worst place to sit on a twelve-hour flight.

The flight attendant walked over and handed me my passport. "Um, here you go," she said, and I laughed and thanked her.

Holding my passport again on that almost-empty plane, I understood, in a way, how lucky I had been. The passport hadn't been confiscated. I was not imprisoned. And yet, this was how Israel treated someone with a voice and American citizenship. There are today, held without charge in the Israeli military detention system, hundreds of Palestinian children. There are reports of a systematic pattern of ill treatment toward them. Silenced and oppressed, these prisoners have little recourse. In the news recently I saw that two thousand of these prisoners have resorted to the last form of protest left to them: they have collectively gone on hunger strike.

I flipped through the passport and, surprised, found that

the officials had left a stamp on it. The stamp was massive and read, in English and Hebrew, *Ben Gurion Airport EN-TRY DENIED*. I stared at it for a few minutes. Then, I saw it: the picture of the ship I had seen eight hours earlier, that I had thought was a sign of good luck.

I remembered how, when I first met my ex's stepmother in Texas, we had bonded over her collection of costume jewelry. A lot of the pieces were from her first husband, whom she had divorced before meeting my then-father-in-law. I noticed that many of the pieces he'd given her had imagery of boats and ships. When I pointed that out to her, she had raised her wine glass and said, "You're right! He was shippin' me out." And that's what had happened to me. I had been shipped out.

Two massive, bald-headed men sat on either side of me. If I believed the conspiracies, I would have thought those guys were Mossad. But it was obvious before long, from the way they blasted terrible club music on their earphones and, later, passed out, that they were just some doofuses on their way to America. In an attempt to be polite and not touch the men around me, I folded my arms, but this became terribly uncomfortable after a while. A few hours into our flight, I decided that I was tired of being polite and so I put both my arms down. Minutes later, the man on my right began to jab my elbow. I ignored him and feigned sleep. He jabbed and jabbed.

Finally, I turned to him, my arm firmly on the armrest, and said, "I get it."

He looked at me, embarrassed.

"I really get it. But I am keeping this armrest. I am not moving. I will keep my arm here for the rest of the flight," I said. And I did.

17

BIBLIOCLAST

My father. He wanted me to be a writer, but when I became one, he didn't like what I wrote.

I didn't speak to him for almost seven years after I published my first novel, which he hated and called pornography: it features lots of teenage sex and masturbation, as well as an unsavory portrayal of a narcissistic and selfish father. He insisted it was the sex scenes that offended him—and not the depiction of the father character, who had been very, very loosely based on him. My father said he would only speak to me again if I publicly burned every single copy of my book. I love imagining myself doing this, my transformation from rejected pornographer to redeemed daughter and biblioclast.

•

Most texts are burned because they are deemed, by one religious group or another, as being heretical.

Torah scrolls were burned by ancient Romans. The Talmud was burned in medieval France. The Quran was burned in the United States. In 2010 a pastor named Terry Jones threatened to burn two hundred Qurans on the ninth anniversary of 9/11. He didn't do it, but dozens of Qurans were set on fire on September 11 by other people (all men; biblioclasts are overwhelmingly male).

My novel was a heretical text, too—in our household, my father was God, and his word was Truth, and anyone who talked back to him, or even just interrupted him during breakfast, was a heretic whose book needed to be burned.

•

I've started indulging in this fantasy of myself as a biblioclast. Here is what I imagine:

I round up all the copies of the book in my house. I have two paperbacks in my office, six hardcovers in an old chest, and two advance reader copies on a shelf in the dining room. If it is summer in my imagination, I burn them in my backyard in the barbecue pit; if it is winter, I burn them in my fireplace.

Next I begin to contact readers who might have copies. I ask them to mail all the copies to a post office box in Kyle,

Texas—the town in which I began writing the novel, when I lived in a trailer for three hundred dollars a month (including all utilities). The readers, baffled, comply, because I explicitly state to them how important it is for my father that I do this. Friends who have heard my complaints about my father—that he was so strict I wasn't allowed to socialize; that he struck me; that he often made me feel as if my large body was unworthy of love—don't understand why I would burn all my books for him. I tell them that my father did his best to love me; that he praised my writing; that he took me on a trip to New York City when I was thirteen; that he used to sing with me and laugh at my jokes. I tell my friends that now, as I near the age of forty, and work in a place where I am a minority, my empathy for him has deepened, that I can finally imagine what it must have been like for him, a Palestinian, to immigrate to the U.S. and work at a job where he was the only Arab, perhaps the only person of color. I tell them that I miss my father, and it becomes a bit easier for them to understand.

•

The Quran was orally passed on in the years after the Prophet Muhammad's death, and it was not written down until two decades later (between 650 and 656). In Arabic the slightest mispronunciation can change the meaning of a word entirely. (When my father was a boy and heard the muezzin's call to prayer, "Hayya ala salaa," he thought the word *hayya*, which means *come*, was the same as the word *hayya*, which means *snake*, and so he would imagine a snake on a prayer rug, which confused him greatly.)

After the Quran was fully transcribed, the caliph ordered that all manuscripts containing any verses or excerpts from the Quran be burned, so that there would be only one official version.

I always wondered how the versions learned by heart, the ones that differed from the official Quran, could be destroyed. How do you erase memory?

•

In my biblioclast fantasy, I order every single copy of my book from bookstores and warehouses around the country.

Then the tricky part: the book is in several public and college libraries. This is when things get illegal.

I check out every single copy of my book through interlibrary loans, and if that's not possible, I fly out to the libraries and steal the copies. If I can't steal the copies, I set fire to them in the library bathrooms and try to escape before the fire alarm goes off.

Now the expensive part: the copies of my book in China, in Taiwan, in Italy, in Germany, in Palestine. I ask readers for help burning the books, but they can only do so much. So I purchase a multicity plane ticket:

FAT–Berlin–Rome–Beijing–Taipei–AUS

I don't bother to fly to Tel Aviv. I call a friend of mine,

a journalist, and she rounds up all the Hebrew copies and burns them in front of a settlement that had once burned down her family's olive orchard, and she takes photos of the whole thing so we can show proof to my father that those copies are burned.

I go on my multicity trip. In Berlin, I snort coke and go clubbing for forty-two hours straight, and at the end of it, I drunkenly collect all the German copies of my book in a sack and carry it onto a flight to Rome, where I drink lots of espresso and do the same thing all over again. I find every copy of my book in China, and in Taiwan, too. I take all these copies with me on a flight from Taipei to Austin.

When I arrive in Austin, I get nostalgic, because I can't afford to live there anymore. The airport is full of transplants, cowboy-boot-wearing women who don't deserve to live there. I rent a car and drive twenty miles to Kyle, Texas; go to the post office where the rest of the books wait for me; and take them all to a field a few miles out of town by the five-mile dam where my son and I used to swim because it was free. I pile the books into a kind of pyre, a paper ziggurat. In my hand I carry long, dramatic matches. My best friend stands with me and asks me if I'm sure I want to do this, and I say I do, because despite everything I love my dad. Then I light a match and touch its bald, burning red head to the base of the pyre.

The books go up in blue flames. The flames last for a while. The biblioclasm gives me a small bibliogasm. I take pictures with my iPhone and text them to my mother so she can show them to my father. After an hour of burning, I check my email on my iPhone. I have three junk emails from Netflix, PEN America, and Change.org.

A few minutes later, my mother texts and says that my father wants to know if I also deleted all the files of the book on my computer.

I sprint to my house in California from the field in Texas, and a few minutes later pull up all the files on my laptop. I delete them. Then I find the novel files I had sent myself as backups in 2001, 2003, 2004, 2005. I delete those, too. Every single trace of my first novel is deleted.

•

In 2003, after the U.S. invasion of Iraq, fires ravaged the Iraqi National Library and Archive, the Library of Religious Endowments, the library of the University of Baghdad's college of fine arts, and one called House of Wisdom. The buildings were bombed or set aflame by looters. Iraq had lost its libraries in many wars before; in the thirteenth century, all of Iraq's libraries were burned down, including the original House of Wisdom. It was said that the water of the Tigris River ran indigo with the ink of books that had been hurled into it.

•

My first book is completely erased.

That's when I imagine my father arriving at my rented

bungalow to tell me he loves me again. We hug. After we hug, he tells me he noticed, while we were hugging, that I have back rolls, and that my skin is dry, and that, if I really loved him, I would lose weight.

Shrink.

Become smaller and smaller.

And that's when I have to admit to myself that my father might want *me* to disappear. He might want to erase me. To throw me and not my book onto the pyre.

•

In 1948, Israeli soldiers ransacked Palestinian homes and looted family libraries. Sixty thousand books and manuscripts were stolen. The eight thousand books that remain are now housed at the National Library of Israel. The other fifty-two thousand books were burned or recycled. My father was burned—no, born!—in 1950, and he grew up in the West Bank. Like all Palestinians, his biggest crime was his birth, and the sentence of this crime is disappearance. The main problem with Palestinians is that they continue to exist.

In 2007, the Hamas-run Ministry of Education threatened to burn a collection of Palestinian folklore because it was pornographic. But Palestinians protested this decision, saying the folktales were sometimes crude, but they were also a cultural treasure. They'd been transmitted orally for centuries before being written down. They needed to be preserved. The ministry swiftly revoked the decision to set the books aflame.

•

Recently I met an elderly artist whose daughter didn't talk to him for years. We sat together by a natural pool and he told me that he thinks my father wants me to respect him. It began to rain. He told me that sometimes we have to apologize to the people who wronged us.

Another man, M, told me that having a father is better than not having a father. His own father died six years ago.

Then a good friend of mine lost her father.

And that is when I decided to contact my father—for real—to see if he still wants me to burn my books.

He doesn't.

I fly out to New York to see him, and when we meet, I apologize. I tell him I'm sorry that I hurt him. We hug. Seven years have passed. We are both on our best behavior. He isn't critical of me; however, he doesn't apologize in return. I ask if we can agree not to talk about the hurtful things we've said and done in the past. Yes, he says, let's not mention the times you've shamed and disappointed me. He laughs, and I try to laugh, too.

That afternoon we go for a walk and stop at the shop that carries his favorite Arabic newspaper. He buys it, and I hug him again while he holds the newspaper that is written in his mother tongue.

My father is now a man with Parkinson's, his body slightly curled downward, his socks pulled up too high, his mustache completely white. Seeing him this changed, this transformed, stings. And I finally understand that I need to let go of my old image of my father—the man who is a tyrant, bully, and biblioclast. Because that man no longer exists.

18

YES AGAIN, GODDESS

This is the way I had originally ended that last chapter:

My first book is completely erased.

That's when I imagine my father arriving at my rented bungalow to tell me he loves me again. We hug. After we hug, he tells me he noticed, while we were hugging, that I have back rolls, and that my skin is dry, and that, if I really loved him, I would lose weight.

Shrink.

Become smaller and smaller.

And that's when I have to admit to myself that my father

might want me to disappear. He might want to erase me. To throw me and not my book onto the pyre.

I go to my son's room. He has a copy of my novel that I gave him when he was twelve years old. I find it on his desk. I take it out to the living room, where my father is standing, and I throw it at him. And this makes him dissolve from my life completely, sending him back to his own house. All that remains of him is a single facial hair, which floats, left, and then right, and back again, down to the wood floor, a hair that I will mop up eventually and flush down the drain, water finally putting out the origins of fire.

I had written it that way because I hadn't yet reached out to him, hadn't yet found that small space inside me to forgive him.

•

M, my young ex-lover, had been the one who'd encouraged me to contact my father. He said that one of us was going to have to bend, and that since I was the younger one, it would have to be me. I resisted this for a short while. Then I put feelers out to my mother and my brother and sister, to see if they thought he'd be open to it.

During this time, I also met an Egyptian man who was interested in kink.

The shift from M to this other man is important because the other man is the one that held my hand over the threshold of becoming dominant in bed. M helped—by opening me up to role-play, kinky acts such as adult nursing, ball hitting, flogging, and more.

I mention this here, while I write about my father, because I am aware that, for myself in particular, my father's fear of my sexuality, his instructions to me to remain a virgin, his expectations of my femininity or what he perceived as a lack thereof—all of these were twinned, in practice, with his abuse of me. For sixteen years, he hit me. My first memory is of him taking me out of bed when I was eighteen months old, placing me on the floor behind the living room couch, and hitting me. Sexuality, pain, love, obedience, hurt: all are woven together in the loom that is my body, that is my skin and my heart.

•

In 2007, my father visited me in Michigan with my mother. My sister and brother also met us there, and we all stayed at my house, a place I was renting for an amount below market thanks to a friend of a friend, who had helped me find it. I was in Michigan for graduate school, and the house was a dream— three bedrooms, with an additional writing nook in my room. There was a washer and dryer in the basement. There was a basement. My son was ten when we moved, and it was the first house we ever lived in together that wasn't my parents'.

My sister, who was finishing her undergraduate studies at the time, understood what a big deal this was, and she cried when she came up to the second floor of the house and hugged me. She said she was so relieved that I had a home, a place I could write and raise my child. I was thrilled. We held hands and walked downtown and looked at comic books and drank hot chocolate together, and she and my son played with some toys on the living room floor.

I had received the first payment for my first novel from the publisher, and I spent it on a perfect mattress and a wooden sleigh bed. They arrived the day before my parents did. My son and I put clean sheets on for my parents and napped in the bed. The next day, they showed up and nothing in the house was good enough for my dad. Every hotel and motel in the area was sold out thanks to a football game—a sport my family never watched or talked about. My parents were stuck in my house. At some point, my father told me I was fat and that I would probably be immobile by the age of fifty. I cried and left.

My father grew up in a shack on the side of a mountain, in the West Bank, and fled at age seventeen. He lived in a hostel in Jordan and smoked cigarettes for a year. When the Egyptian president made education free to all exiled Palestinians, my father joined his brother in Alexandria, where he lived and studied engineering in the late sixties and through the seventies. He met famous poets and novelists and playwrights, wrote poetry, and wooed my knotty-haired mama, a soft-spoken pianist.

In one of our family photos, we are at a café in Alexandria and my baba is presenting my diapered body to Tawfiq el-Hakim, the Arab world's Molière, Chekhov, Proust, and Ibsen all rolled into one. Years later, when I enrolled in a

Middle Eastern studies program, I discovered that el-Hakim was a huge misogynist whose female characters have no agency and no positive traits. I wanted to call my father and tell him this but was afraid he would hang up on me.

My father always wanted me to be a writer. When I showed promise in dance and music, he shook his head and said, "Who wants to be a singer when you can be a novelist?" I did, but that didn't matter. I was meant to write a novel about the history of my family and our struggles. That's what my father always told me.

In the photo, his body was still svelte and solid. My father had, alongside his outward obsession with writers, a secret obsession with his body. He spent my childhood on diets and exercise regimens. When I was a child, he went off to "fat farms" and came back pounds slimmer. I thought all men were like this until I left home. Even after I succeeded at writing and publishing, my father was obsessed with my size.

•

During their visit to my new house in Michigan, I took my father and mother to a public library whose architecture I was sure my father would admire. We sat at a table and flipped through journals, and he asked me if I saw myself as beautiful. When I said I did, he told me I was wrong. I got up and left in tears. A week later, I saw a man my father's age sitting in the same seat by the new-fiction collection. I had to resist the urge to ask him if he thought I was pretty.

After my family left the house, peace came over me again.

But later that month, I found one of my dad's white undershirts in the basement, where I did my laundry. I was so angry with him that I felt a seething hatred, and I threw the shirt on the basement floor. I stomped on it, spat on it, picked it up and ripped it at the sleeves. I threw it back down and spat on it and stood on it. I wanted to be the one beating *him* up in a basement. I wanted to win, to be strong, to overpower all his judgments and violence and pain.

A little over ten years later, I was back in my parents' home, standing in their basement and doing a load of my parents' laundry. I was standing right by the water heater, right by the spot where my father had beaten me twenty-four years earlier. He was upstairs now, his left leg slightly shaking, his bones bruised from his disease, his hands curled in his lap. I laundered his undershirts and socks and my mother's things happily, wanting to help. For some reason, there was a baseball bat just a couple of feet from the washing machine. I wanted to feel something, anger, bitterness, revenge, self-pity—anything at all. But all I could feel was sadness, both for the man my father used to be and for the powerless girl I once was. It was perhaps the seven years that I spent away from him that helped me reach this destination in myself. The fact that by the end of the seven years, every cell in each of our bodies had turned and changed, so that not a single part of him had ever beaten me, and not a single part of myself had ever been beaten.

19

BAD MUSLIM

I'd been in bed with a married man when I realized that my own marriage was over.

I was leaning over his body when an odd feeling of nostalgia took hold of me. It was a bit too soon to be nostalgic, but I couldn't help it, my sense of nostalgia: it was genetic. For a moment, I thought of how my husband and I used to spend hours at this, when we first met, of how my husband hadn't had sex with me in over a year. And I thought, looking down at the married man, this is what people talk about when they say that as soon as you start thinking about the beginning of a relationship, you've reached the end.

I had spent the afternoon with the married man by a lake. The lake glittered, and the married man told me, as we sat by a fire at the edge of the lake, that he had heard the lake was so deep that it could flood the entire state. He made a motion with his hands to show how deep into the earth the lake was; late that night, he made that same gesture as his fingers went in and out of me.

There were casinos near the lake, and before his hands went in and out of me, he said he wanted to gamble. I walked through a small wood and to the hotel near my cabin, and I saw him at the bar of the hotel casino; he was already very drunk. I told him I wasn't sure I would gamble, but that I would watch him. He wanted to know why I didn't want to gamble, and I told him it was the last thing forbidden in Islam that I hadn't broken, the only thing I had left to call myself a Muslim by. I ate pork, didn't pray, never fasted Ramadan, and had sex. But gambling, I said, I had never gambled.

This must have turned the married man on, because he became determined that I should gamble. He put his hands on my shoulders and said, "We are going to gamble."

I had lied to him about never gambling. I had gambled with my best friend in Louisiana; five of us had driven out there from Texas in 2005 and for her bachelorette party we gambled all night, and then slept in a double motel room, drunk.

I had lied to him because I knew it would turn him on, the notion of taking my gambler cherry, stripping me of being a Muslim. And it worked. He gave the blackjack dealer two hundred dollars and split the chips into two piles, pushing one of the piles to me. I had never played blackjack—that part was true—but he taught me patiently. He told me when to hit and when to stay. The dealer, a middle-aged brunette named Jill, assumed we were a couple. I told her we were in town for our twelfth anniversary. The married man glanced at me; he played along.

When we ran out of chips, he put another hundred on the table, split the chips again.

The casino played the Rolling Stones, and I said, I fucking hate this song. I want to get what I want.

The truth was, though I had gambled before, I had never cheated on a husband. I had been living without regular sex for years, and yet, I had never cheated. *Zina* was the Arabic word in the Quran for *adultery*. It was a beautiful word, the *z* so final, the *a* at the end feminine, bewitching. So though I didn't pop my gambler cherry that night, I popped my infidelity cherry; my zina cherry.

When I got blackjack, the married man leaned in and kissed me. He loved that I was being a bad Muslim.

●

When I was a child, I flared up with fevers and strep at least once or twice a year. My mother would come to my bed and put cold compresses on my forehead and then pat me with the back of her hand, her wrists encircled with bracelets her father had given her when she had graduated from college—the first woman in her family to do so. She would pet my forehead and read, in a whisper, verses from the Quran. My favorite was the verse about envy and evil, with its images of witches blowing on knots. She read the verse over and over, soothing my fever and my skin, nursing me back to health.

As an adult woman, I tried to fast Ramadan, to pray five times a day, to give alms to the poor, to read up on my rights as a wife. I only succeeded at the latter. I discovered, early on in my marriage, that a wife is entitled to sex with her husband at least once every four months. A husband who doesn't provide sex for his wife is sinning by denying her. I tried to talk about this with my mother once but was too shy; I wanted to talk to all my friends about my sexless marriage but was too ashamed. And besides: my husband wasn't Muslim.

•

I did not meet the married man by the lake. The first time I met him, the very first time, was on a train from Hamburg, Germany, to Berlin. I was on my German book tour and he boarded the train one stop after I did. He was wearing denim and a cashmere scarf and a hat. He was helping a fellow passenger with a guitar case; I got up to help them both, but mostly to place myself in view of the man, because I was so drawn to him. I asked him if he was a musician, and he said he was a writer and told me his name. I recognized it but pretended I didn't. He asked me if I was a singer. I said I wasn't. I said I was a writer, and that I was touring Germany with my book in translation. He said he was touring Germany with his book, too.

He invited me to join him two rows back. I glanced at the woman seated next to me; her face was contorted with disgust at my loud voice. She had been disgusted since I sat next to her, repulsed by my fat body. The married man was not repulsed by me, and I got up and went to sit next to him. I sat across the aisle because a woman—his publicist, I found out later—was sitting directly next to him.

The man and I both wore wedding rings. We had both lived in the same small college town once. He told me about the time a man had held him at knifepoint outside a bar. He told me about his twenties, immigrating to America, his attempt to be a teacher before he became a writer. The college town had given him refuge the way it had given me refuge. My son and me. We spoke about our children.

We talked the entire ride over to Berlin, and when the train stopped, he invited me to go to his reading that evening and said he would put my name on the list at the box office. I told him I was already an invitee at the same literary festival, and was already on the list. Amusingly, or perhaps because he was blindly sexist, he ignored me and kissed my cheek and said he hoped to see me later.

I walked around Berlin completely adrift and bored and lonely. There was nothing that could wick away the moisture that such an intense encounter had created. I was swimming in it. I needed him. I wanted to keep hearing his voice, his stories.

I met with my publicist and she told me she was going to the festival venue, so I told her the married man had asked me to see him read, and she whooped, because the married man had written books she admired. I walked with her to the venue and got in with my festival-writer pass, and I found the married man immediately, in the grass outside, smoking a cigarette. I was too nervous to approach him. Plus, I wanted him to miss me a little.

I walked and sat in the hall for his reading. He read and spoke for forty-five minutes. Afterward, when he saw me, he walked right up to me, put his hand on the small of my back, and kissed the corner of my mouth. He asked me to hang by and go for dinner afterward. I waited thirty minutes but then decided not to stay near him anymore. I was married. I had only been with my husband a total of three years, one of them married. We hadn't had sex in months, but I was hopeful that would change. It was Ramadan. I walked out of the venue and didn't say goodbye to anyone, just walked away and through a park and into a small market and then back to my hotel. I ordered a bloody steak sandwich and ate it and then sopped up the blood with the bread and thought about fucking the married man, went to bed, and in the morning, left Berlin.

When I got home, my husband still would not have sex with me. For a year, he didn't have sex with me. We went to therapy, and the therapist said that we needed to create a nightly touching practice where we lay in bed, side to side, and petted each other without necessarily doing anything sexual at all. Soon enough, I was begging him to keep up the practice with me. He wasn't only refusing to have sex with me; he was refusing to settle into the nightly touching, too. When I nagged him to pet me, I felt I'd become removed from my original desire: that he fuck me. This made me angry, but because I believed that my large body wasn't lovable, I didn't leave.

When the married man and I left the casino, and went to his cabin, and when he asked me what I wanted to do, I said, Anything you want to do.

The married man then drew me a bath and told me to get in. I put my lips on his, something I'd wanted to do years before, on the train to Berlin. He didn't kiss me back, testing me. I waited, my mouth completely still, until, finally, he reached for my tongue with his. He twisted my hair in his hands, then pulled roughly. It hurt, but I told myself I needed to take it. I undressed and he watched, then said Wow when I was done. I was scared he said it because I was fat. My husband hadn't told me I was fat in years, but I knew he still thought it. I got in the tub, floated back, allowed my breasts to peek out. He didn't want to undress; he stood at the edge of the tub and washed me, pleasured me. He rubbed my feet clean, then sucked my toes. I took his hands and put them over my throat gently, playing at force. He choked me. I was afraid. He let go. I took a deep breath, and when I let it out, he choked me again and held me underwater. I thought I would die.

I struggled, and he let go.

I wanted to ask him to stop but didn't know how. He slapped my breasts, my belly. He asked me to slap his face.

I did. I slapped him harder and harder. He was soaked in water, his hands around my neck. He hit me on the head. Harder and harder. I finally said Stop. He stopped. He took out his penis. It was small, and I was disappointed and embarrassed for him. I was embarrassed that he'd hit me and embarrassed that his dick was so small. I got out of the tub and got into his bed. He put his hand on my vulva and roughly fingered me, harder than I wanted, and I understood that it was because he couldn't roughly fuck me. He fell asleep when I put him in my mouth. I got out of bed and found his wallet and his credit cards all over the floors of the cabin. I took out receipts from his wallet and read them: a burrito he'd eaten in Manhattan, a meal he'd bought his children. I wanted proof that he'd hurt me and that I'd spent this night with him. I texted a mutual acquaintance and asked her to pick me up from the married man's cabin in the morning. I got back into bed and tried to sleep.

When I woke up, he asked, proud, if I felt sore. I said I didn't, even when I felt the bruises. I didn't want him to think he'd hurt me, broken me. I had the bruises on my neck and breasts for over a week afterward; they were a yellowish hue when I finally left my husband, who didn't notice them.

•

I left my husband after I came home from the lake. I told him it was over while we were in bed. He had made love to me three times in five years and refused to get help. This convinced me that there was nothing wrong with him, that he was simply not attracted to me.

He packed all his things and left two weeks later, and he took half of our books. It felt almost as if the books' absence was also the absence of his body, and this made me very sad.

•

My mother called, after I told her that I left my husband. She wanted to help me through my sadness, but I declined her calls. She had told me once, when I had confided in her years earlier about how I often felt hopeless and depressed, that I should pray. She said that praying and talking to God would help me feel better. I have maybe seen my mother pray once or twice my entire life. I wanted to tell her what I had read once: that my husband was the one who had sinned. That he'd been depriving me of my rights.

The next Ramadan after my divorce, I thought once again of the married man and of the way my skin felt for days after that night I committed zina for the first and only time; it felt as if the married man's hands were still on me, this strange other, the one I'd invited to heal me, to help hurt me and release me, all at once.

20

LOVE IS NEITHER SLAVE NOR PHARAOH

Many women claim that, because they are bosses out in the real world, constantly fighting to be heard, respected, understood, and obeyed, they want to be the opposite in bed: submissive, taken care of, coddled, made to obey, made to respect, made to listen.

In my conversations with other women, when I've asked them if they've ever been the dominant one, they often said they had no interest. Then I met E.

A disabled poet and a badass, she dominated her husband from across rooms with a remote-controlled device, which sent shock signals to a cock ring, which she'd placed around his balls in the morning. He begged her to do this to him. The differences in the size of their bodies painted them as inverses of each other; he was large and tall, she was petite and short, and in the real world, she was the one forced to deal with people's assumptions about her diminutive body, its supposed disenfranchisement, lack of power, weakness.

We were in a bar when she asked me what my favorite domme activities were. At that point, I had never dommed anyone. I told her so, and she widened her eyes in surprise. Then, excitedly, she told me about her own rituals and experiences. I listened, her tutee, grateful to her for the trust she'd placed in me. She told me about the ball torture device; the many floggers and whips she had hung up near her bed; the sounding device she inserted into her husband's urethra. I went back to my place that afternoon and researched tools of torture late into the night.

And over the next six months, I slowly began purchasing them. I bought a pair of leather gloves, which I used to slap M's cock if it didn't stand at attention for me. I bought a dick leash, which I fastened at the base of his dick while parading him around the house, calling him a worthless dog. But I had yet to feel the power E had told me of, the power and joy of being called a goddess. I yearned to find a partner who would want that, too.

•

I learned the practical and hands-on experiences of being a domme with A, the lover I met while I was with M. He was thirty-two, Egyptian, and Muslim. A would come over once a week and stand by my leather couch. He waited for my command. I'd sit in a big armchair and tell him to take all his clothes off. I would tell him to sit at my feet, on his knees. He did what I asked. I told him to lick my boots. He asked if this was hygienic. A was afraid of germs. This put him in a bit of a pickle since he was also very much a slave. I told him to shut the fuck up and lick my boots. He did, and then he took them off and held my feet in his hands. His hands trembled.

I met A on Tinder. He was looking for a dominant woman to step on his cock. I was looking for a submissive man who would let me step on his cock. Soon, he was sitting on the wood floor right across from my chair, on a chain attached to my foot. My foot on his balls.

A asked if I want to hear Egyptian music. I said yes.

I told him that earlier that week, I had bumped into a man who had asked me to think of all the Egyptians I knew. "Aren't they either slaves or pharaohs?" This question made me uncomfortable, especially since it was asking for an absolute judgment about a specific ethnic background. By saying that people were either in charge or subservient, he wasn't taking into account all the subtleties of power dynamics, of how a submissive person can wield control, of how a pharaoh-like person attains and earns authority.

I asked A what he thought of this theory. He said, "I only

know what I like and cannot speak for all Egyptian men."
I liked that about him. Not so eager to generalize. Plus, he
wanted to be special.

And so A would sit on my floor, a collar around his neck,
a leash hooked onto his collar. He would have his laptop
open, too, and work on a lesson plan for his classes the following day. It occurred to me to ask him if he wanted some
tea. But I didn't want to get up and make it. Besides, he was
my sub—he was supposed to make my tea. I wanted to lean
in, unhook his collar, and send him into the kitchen to boil
water for my tea. If he were white, I would have done it in an
instant. But he was Arab, his hair kinky, his skin the color of
my mother's skin, my son's skin, and it took more gumption
for me to dominate him—to domme him around. He told me
that his previous dommes were all white. The image of him
on a chain at the feet of a white woman infuriates me. Haven't
Arab and Muslim men had enough of being chastised, dominated, humiliated, and incarcerated by white supremacy?

I didn't ask him this question because it would further
upset me if he responded that he didn't mind it. Instead, I
told him he was never allowed to serve anyone else but me,
and he lowered his gaze like a good Muslim and said, "Yes,
goddess."

I unhooked his collar and told him to go make me some
tea. He walked to the kitchen naked and put the electric kettle on and came back. A few minutes later, when the teakettle
clicked off, I led him by the leash to the kitchen and showed
him where the spoons were, where the honey was, and how

to measure out my black tea leaves. He did, and then we returned to the bedroom, to work. A couple of minutes later, he got on his hands and knees, and I placed my tea cup on the small of his lower back and poured myself a cup. A liked it when I treated him like furniture. I loved that in my room, with his consent, I could treat a man like furniture.

The next morning, distracted by the thought of him making me tea, by the thought of his naked body, I filled the electric kettle with water, placed it on the gas stove, and lit the stove. It took a moment for me to realize what I had done, and I turned off the stove and checked the bottom of the kettle for damage. There was none. Afterward, the smoke alarm beeped.

•

My experiences with pain during sex were all negative before BDSM. The pain was never consensual. Men gagged me, thinking I enjoyed it. They bit my nipples, assuming that because my breasts were large, they were stronger and impervious to pain. They choked me, their hands over my throat, because I asked them to, but none of them had done any training to figure out how to do it correctly, responsibly. Until BDSM, a lot of sex felt like assault. With BDSM, limits are discussed; classes on bondage, rope tying, slapping, choking, and anything else are offered at different "dungeons," clubs, and other spaces. It's almost the sex education everyone should be able to have. I often wish it were.

•

When I was a little girl, around five or six, one of my favorite things to do was to play a game I called "motorcycle." I would beg my brother, or my cousin, or a neighbor, to lie on his back with his legs stretched straight up. I'd grip his ankles and pretend that the legs were the metal arms of a motorcycle, and then I'd place my foot on his testicles and pretend that they were a gas pedal. I had no idea that I was stepping on testicles, only that they were soft like a small jellyfish and felt funny under my feet.

I told this story to A when we first met up. His response was "Lucky boys!" He derived no pleasure at all from his penis being stroked or touched. All he wanted to do was please me. His hands quivered when I first allowed him to touch me. I'd never seen or heard a man behave so dutifully, so adoringly. He called me his goddess. I told him to kiss me from head to toe, and he complied, his breath quickening. He loved pleasing me. It's all he wanted to do.

I penetrated his mouth and his ass, because I wanted to, and he wanted to do anything I wanted to do.

I understood right away that being in charge of him was a huge responsibility. I had to make sure that when he was gagging, he wasn't really hurt. I had to make sure his breath wasn't restricted if I smothered him with my breasts. Before we did anything, we had very long discussions over text about what he would and would not consent to. This openness, these clear boundaries, felt nothing like vanilla dating or vanilla sex. It was the vanilla stuff that was scary, I finally understood: often unnegotiated or under-communicated. How many times had I been assaulted in one way or another during vanilla sex? Countless. There was the woman who fisted me against my will; the man who thought my gagging sounds were fun; the guys who thought it was fine to slap my ass without asking permission.

With BDSM, nothing "just happened." Every action, desire, and movement was discussed beforehand. "Please never make me eat my cum," A had said. "Please never pierce my skin, or make me bleed, or hit my body. Only my face."

Kink meant consent, always. It meant a discussion of boundaries, desires, fears. Unlike vanilla hookups, it meant safety. It meant true submission.

•

A slowly stopped responding to my texts after a few months of seeing each other. The silent weeks would be followed by days of ardent messages, begging for my attention. When I gave it, he disappeared again. He was married, it turned out, and I told him that there was no room in our female-dominated relationship for deceit or polytheism. I was a monotheistic-type goddess. When I broke things off with him, I felt a deep sadness. A was the first good, responsive, and devoted lover I had who, like me, also had a Muslim identity. This shared background made me feel safe, healed me of the years I thought my mother was a pushover, the years of internalized Islamophobia, years that I thought Muslim men were too rigid or stubborn or proud to submit to anyone but God.

I believed I would never find another Muslim person to be kinky with.

•

I met Z a year after I met A, almost to the day. We both serendipitously wore red-and-white-striped tops to our first date. I loved this because we looked like a Muslim version of *Where's Waldo?* Where's Habibi? I had often thought. We talked about everything, including whether kink was in the Quran. "When the Quran says to beat or whip someone, it never says how hard," he said, joking. "Maybe it's soft play."

Z told me he was hit by a train when he was twenty-three. When I asked him how that happened, he said it was because he and his friends were playing chicken with the train. I wanted to tell him how stupid that was, but instead, I asked him if it was something he did regularly: play chicken with the train. He said yes. He did it all the time. He said that the time he was hit was the only time he paused to think about the train hitting him. He said he blames being hit on that pause. The train hit him, and he spun in place, like a dreidel. He spun and spun before he hit the ground. The spinning absorbed a lot of the contact, so that when he hit the ground, he wasn't too severely injured. He was airlifted to a hospital. Four years later, he was diagnosed with testicular cancer. He has one ball. I pull on it gently when he's in my mouth to help him cum.

Z's Islam was, like mine, more of an identity than a practice. We spent the first day of Ramadan getting stoned and driving forty-five miles out of town to attend a LARP, or a live-action role-play game, where nerds gather in large spaces and pretend to be vampires. We arrived too early, and I began jerking him off in the car, a mile away from the exit. We ended up fucking in a parking lot for half an hour, him calling me his good girl. At the end of Ramadan, he came over, and we drank Eid champagne. We pretended that the label read "Halal. Enjoy for Eid!" In the morning, I asked him if he thought the pork chorizo I had in the fridge was bad. He smelled it and said he didn't know. I told him I didn't know anything about pork. He said he didn't either, and we laughed. Two Muslims trying to make eggs and chorizo? It didn't happen.

•

The first time I asked Z to collar me, I was nervous. I didn't want to be rejected. But I trusted him; we had been playing for five months, and I knew I would be safe if I went into submission with him. He said yes. So I brought out A's collar, which is black leather with red floral stitching, and we stood facing each other. I threw a pillow on my wood floors, the floors A once licked my feet on, and got on my knees. I asked Z if I could look at him, and he said, "Yes." I looked up and he fastened the collar on me, gently, and then hooked the leash onto the metal circle. I breathed deeply. It was a relief to finally be the one taken care of. To not constantly be working to ensure a sub's safety. It was finally my turn to let go.

21

TAKING THE KNIFE

A year later, I found a dungeon that hosted events that were exclusively queer. Most attendees were of color, and I would walk in to the sounds of slaps, moans, and laughter. L, the doorboi, was usually dressed in slacks, a dress shirt, and a black tie. One night, they told me I could walk right in, but to be prepared that Mx C was being fucked with knives. L was biracial and had a side shave, roots dark and curls bleached blond and haloing their face. They were a bratty bottom and a commanding presence. I trusted L more than any cisgendered dude bouncer. They asked me to leave my belongings in the coat closet and welcomed me in.

Beyond the front waiting room was the loft, decked out in gear: a St. Andrew's cross, glowing red and black; a spanking horse bench; a large bird cage; a white four-poster bed; hooks hanging from the ceiling; a padded bench with a cage locked underneath it. Someone was curled in there, sucking a lollipop.

When L had said that Mx C was being fucked by knives, I had no actual idea that they meant it literally. C was spread on a bench while a butch daddy stood between her legs, holding a large play knife, and pumping it in C's pussy. I was standing behind C so I couldn't tell if this was really happening. There was a crowd cheering on the scene—all women, mostly of color. The domme yelled at us, saying we were missing the whole view. A few of us moved over and sat on or around a bench just a few feet from C. We could see the knife pumping into C. I told myself that the knife was dull. It was flat and glinting. I kept looking to see what the trick was, the way I had once when I saw a magician sawing a woman in half at the Magic Castle (a kinky but awful dungeon in its own ways). C was orgasming. I could tell because her clitoris had enlarged and was bouncing against the silver surface of the knife that was making her cum. When she was done, the domme stopped and untied and held C while we all applauded. She was melting in the domme's arms, enjoying the aftercare. When it got quiet, C sat up blushing, shouted, "Holy fuck!" and jumped off the bench.

•

There is a stereotype that those interested in kink come from abusive families. But the truth is, almost everyone in general is brought up in homes where we were taught to obey our parents without question, and to believe that our bodies belonged to our parents, to the state, to our bosses, or to God. I didn't have a lock on my door until I moved away from my parents' house.

•

No one can touch you here, unless you ask them to. No one can hurt you here, unless you beg them to, negotiating the level of hurt and a safe word, if "stop" does not suffice.

You may not touch anyone here, unless they ask you to. You may not hurt anyone here, unless they beg you to, and negotiate with you the level of hurt and a safe word.

You may ask anyone to touch you and you may ask anyone if you can touch them.

You don't have to touch anyone or be touched by anyone.

You always have the right to say yes, to say no, and to change your mind.

If you don't accept someone's no, you are kicked out immediately.

In kink, consent is queen.

Unlike vanilla sex, consensual kinky sex makes sure each and every party is in negotiation and therefore in control of how much they dish and how much they take. Of all and any levels of pleasure, of pain. For people of color living in 2019 America, this measure of agency and power can mean the world.

•

Great kink busts binaries wide open. Maybe there is not a duality of the self, but a hexagonal? Maybe we have so many desires that we also have just as many selves? Maybe having vanilla, one-on-one, straight sex is also a kink? Maybe we lie to ourselves all the time about what hurts and what doesn't and how much?

Kinky queer sex is playful. All the trauma bonding that was forced on us as children, and that is forced on us now as we navigate and try to protect our bodies in a hateful empire: we can flip that and choose to bond with someone over pain we have both agreed on. Many of the dynamics of being a child are revisited—asking for care, being swaddled, belonging to a crew of neighborhood kids, riding a pony, eating a cake, pinning the tail on a donkey blindfolded, bossing your friend crew around, getting bossed around by your crew, asking your friends to tie you up and pretend to be bandits, tying up a friend and then tickling them—everything is revisited now. And it's all so much better this time around: you are an adult and can give and receive consent.

I cannot imagine a life without kinky queerdo friends of color. Being unable to discuss the dude whose ass I'd fucked the night before. Unable to talk to friends about the woman who I can't stop thinking about, who loves for me to whip her. I need to be able to tell friends that she has the same name as my mother. I need my friends to laugh at this coincidence. To hear me talk about how the woman said, "Touch me everywhere, please," as I tied her wrists and ankles to the ends of the X-shaped cross, her breasts squeezed against it. How I warmed her up first, slapping her butt and skin, then began to crop her from the feet up, increasing the pressure when I got to her thighs. How we fucked on a bench at the back center of the dungeon, even though nobody was fucking yet.

When we were ready to move to a spot to cuddle, and she asked me for aftercare, I brought her to the four-poster bed and held her while everyone around us was fucking, finally. We giggled. I told her I was so glad she was there, and that I'd been worried, since this was my first time at this particular event, that there wouldn't be many people of color. She said she felt the same way, and that she was relieved and excited when she saw me. "When I saw you, I was like, yes! Another South Asian!" I was shocked to hear this; that she knew I was Asian at all, because no one ever does, or considers me that. "Southwest Asian, right?" she said. "Right," I said.

She *saw* me.

Whenever I walked into a dungeon, I breathed more deeply. I felt every moment. I was in the present completely. I had to be: the person I was playing with depended on me and trusted me completely. After cropping someone against a horse bench, helping tie someone to a hook, or spanking someone so hard my palms smarted, I didn't feel gravity as much as I had before. Whenever I left the dungeon, I was completely free of all my chronic pain, of my emotional hunger, of my sadness. I was just me, in that very moment.

•

When I was two days old, the nurses at the Chicago Women's Medical Center asked my parents if they could use me as a model during a bathing demonstration they wanted to share with all the other new parents. My mother and father agreed.

I was held, naked and chubby, in a small yellow tub as two nurses wiped the fat folds of my newly emerged flesh, bathed my downy bottom, and washed my hair.

My mother and father didn't have a baby to wash so they got to watch. For weeks they had been taking child-birth classes in that same hospital, my father giggling as he held my mother and supported her through breath-work exercises.

The reason I used to love the bathing-demonstration story was that in it, I was a body used to show other bodies how to care for bodies like mine. In the story, there was no dangerous knife, and there was no need to be ashamed of my naked body; it would be years before my fat rolls would be deemed repulsive, before being naked in front of a group of people would be unacceptable. Years before I would learn that fat femmes are both hypervisible and invisible. That Muslim femmes are erased or ignored or used as an excuse to invade and decimate entire geographical regions. That if you pose nude, you get death threats from Cairo and get memed as Jabba the Hutt in America.

But I recently learned that two months after my birth and this bathing demo, my parents' childbirth instructor was abducted and assaulted outside this same hospital. She had been taken at gunpoint, bound, and held in her abductor's car trunk; she had knocked against the metal of the trunk in parking lots, but no one was able to help her. The abductor sexually assaulted her, and later murdered her. He was given the death penalty almost two years later, and he died in 1995, years before I would find out that the woman who had helped my mother and father understand how to deliver me to this world was speedily and cruelly delivered out of it by a man who was a rapist and murderer.

•

Again and again, the world reminds me that women are never safe.

When I first started about dungeons, my main preoccupation was with the knife that Mx C was taking. I wanted to explore the ways that kinky sex feels safe while vanilla sex does not. I wanted to really ask myself: what is the knife?

One night, I was invited by a partner to join him at what was billed as a "sex party." When I read the party's rules, I saw that they were mostly suggestions for straight men to behave.

At the party, only two couples were fucking—both straight. One of the men asked me to bring lube from the other room to help his partner be more comfortable. There was no lube. "Well, shit," the man said. "Get in here and help me get her wet." I leaned toward the woman and asked if I could touch her. She didn't respond, and the man kept telling me to touch her. I asked her again. She finally said, "Only him." In that moment, I understood—looking at the man and the way he had tried to consent for someone else—what and where the knife was. What and where real danger was: in all heterosexual non-kinky spaces, where women are in the most danger. Where men think that they can consent for women, and women are dehumanized, silenced, and bound.

•

"Have you ever been chased around your house by a knife?" my partner asked the morning after the party. I told him the story about being sixteen and running from my father holding the knife. He said I told the story so calmly. He wanted to know what healed me from that pain. If anything had. If I was even healed. I asked him why he asked in the first place. I asked him, "Have *you* ever been chased around *your* house by a knife?" He said yes. "I was seven."

He asked me why a mother would hurt her child like that. I asked him why a father would hurt a daughter like that. We held each other and I thought about the dungeon and about Mx C and the knife.

Mx C, spread wide open, chasing the knife with her pussy. Is there even, or can there ever be, a better vision for the kind of love that constantly keeps us, heals us, transforms us, and releases us, cyclically, desperately, longingly, and forever?

22

CITIES VS. WOMEN: A BODY'S SCORECARD

Alexandria 10
To be a girl child
again; to walk
in the streets in
my one-piece,
the color of the
Mediterranean,
a little blue,
polluted, my
hair a red-brown
cloud. To help my
grandfather carry
the umbrella he
will plunge into
the sand at an

angle, rolling the
umbrella in his
palms, shading us
for hours.

Monroe 9
In Monroe, Utah,
I once stayed
in a cabin by a
collection of hot-
springs tubs. The
property was 120
acres large. The
tubs were built
into the rocks,

sulfur spring
water pouring
over the basalt
formations,
boiling hot. My
dog had the runs.
I gave her plenty
of water and
swaddled her in a
makeshift diaper,
in case she got
sick while I was
soaking.
I climbed the
rocky steps up

to the tubs, disrobed, and got in. The sky let the last of the sun's rays dramatically through a thick-gloved cloud, and gazing at it, it made sense that settlers on this land thought God was talking to them. In the tub, I sank deeply as though in a womb.

Fresno 10

My yard had a rose bush. Two, in fact. And fifteen rose trees. It was not *my* backyard, because I didn't own the house, but I tended to it like it was my own. The gazebo that came with the rental once stood in the center, an ominous dark metal cube, and now it was warm, rung with tiny lights, yellow and blue lanterns hanging from each pole, a pink tendrilled plant, a large red tapestry, green and yellow rattan chairs in the middle, a sheesha heavy on a cheap blue rug from Kuwait. My animals circled me, tended to me. The sun was warm, and good. Aretha Franklin was supposed to bail out Angela Davis in 1970. She was stuck in the West Indies and couldn't wire the bail, so a white dairy farmer from Fresno, Rodger McAfee, put his dairy farm and property up as collateral to get Davis out. His children were ostracized in schools.

I had never felt that I belonged to a city or that a city belonged to me. But in Fresno, on the land that freed Angela Davis, I felt that I was at home.

Beirut 5

Three women in niqabs pointed

at me, in a tight red dress and fishnet hose, and laughed. I could not see their faces under the niqabs, but I heard their laughter. Later, young women at the airport laughed at me, too, and the flight attendant asked me to move out of the emergency row. When I asked why, he said, this row is not for the elderly or the sick. I knew where he was going, but I said, I am neither of those things. So he made his shoulders wide and said, You are a very fat person.

I said, And you are incredibly unattractive, but they let you be a flight attendant. I moved to another row so we could take off, and the landscape of Beirut changed beneath me, becoming something less welcoming, something menacing.

Fresno 10
D texted. One line. "Are you two safe?" I asked him why. I did not understand how a man who once beat me wanted to know if I was safe.

He said there was a shooting in Fresno. That the man killed three people. I looked up the shooting and saw that it was a Black man targeting white men, and I was relieved. I told him we were safe, for once, because we weren't white.

Buenos Aires 7
It was sixty-five degrees and sunny every day, but because it was early May, everyone was determined to wear their coats. It was fall. Teenage lovers

kissed each other
on the mouth at
El Ateneo, a belle
epoque theater
turned bookstore.
I walked the
streets from
morning to night
in a light dress,
so when strangers
talked to me, it
was to ask if I
was cold. There
were fully stocked
bars in the
clothing stores in
Palermo, which
I found obscene. I
walked through
the botanical
garden Borges
daydreamed in;
I petted feral
cats. At the
opera house,
the tour guide
asked us where
we were from.

Brooklyn, Berlin,
Istanbul, Chile,
and, I shouted,
Palestine. He said
the tiles we were
walking over
were installed
by Italian
immigrants, and
I looked down
at the Chiclet-
sized white and
red and brown
tiles and saw
young men, their
backs curved Cs,
homesick.

Cairo 3
I stayed in a
hostel in the
middle of
downtown Cairo
the last time
I went before
the revolution.
When I left in
the morning to

buy bread, the
women at the
bakery had to
teach me how to
stand in line and
what to ask for. I
wasn't Egyptian
anymore. Any
Egyptian I had
was solely my
mother, her
labor, her driving
us to and from
the airport in
Alexandria, her
getting us our
ID cards, our
beach permits,
our meals, our
clotheslines;
Mama making
mulokhiya,
lining up for
bread, paying
for taxis, for fish,
for vegetables. I
realized that if
I wanted to stay

Egyptian, I had learn how to do all these things for myself, so I could teach my son, and so on. In the meantime, I was in Cairo, and I was fat and hungry and alone, and all my modest clothes were in an airport somewhere, in a suitcase I'd lost. I left the hostel and went to stay with my childhood friend in Zamalek. There, I was able to walk around a bit more freely, and the street harassment went down to about 50 percent. I bought a pair of jeans and some giant T-shirts from a corner store. My childhood friend told me I was crazy to come to Cairo on vacation. She wanted to know what was wrong with me.

Florence 8

A novelist, two poets, and a composer: we'd been dropped off here by the residency coordinator. Felt as if we were mental-asylum patients, let loose for the day. Spoiled and feeling guilty, I walked across a bridge and took a photo for my son. Later, he would tell me that this was the worst summer of his life. "You weren't there for me, Mom, and I needed you," he'd say. I'd tell him the truth, that I chose six weeks in an Italian artists' residency over him. That sometimes, I am very selfish. That I understood how angry and betrayed he felt, because when I once told my mother that my life from ages fifteen to eighteen was unbearable, that I felt so abused, mistreated, and in pain during that time, and she'd responded, "Those were the best years of my life." I didn't understand her then, but I did now, in Florence, drinking a cocktail, watching a parade invade the square where we sat, actual horses passing a carousel whose colors were the hue of glass-bottled candies.

Oaxaca 3

My son lied and said he could reach the bottom of the ocean. He was ten, and I had taken us to San Agustinillo, a beach town on the coast of Oaxaca. That same year, Aura Goldman drowned a few miles up from the beach where we swam. He said he could reach the bottom, so I swam out to him, but then neither of us could reach the bottom. The tide kept pulling us out. By the shore was a small chapel made of white stone, the virgin of Guadalupe inside it, painted half blue, mourning her son and bowing her head to the god who coerced her to have his child. That's why I've always related to her. My son and I then were being pulled out by the tide, and I began pushing him forward, hoping he'd make it to shore. Finally, I saw a couple on the sand. I'd noticed them earlier—they'd been speaking Hebrew to each other. From the water, I shouted for help, and the couple ran, fast, and got help. They returned with two village men who swam out to my son and me on their boards and carried us to shore. I thanked the Israeli couple and held my kid on the sand.

Istanbul 3

Masha Allah! This is what thin women screeched when they saw me walk past, my size 22 body filling every thread of my blouse and leggings. They laughed when I ate a sandwich outside a restaurant. They only did this when I was alone—when the white women I was staying with walked through Istiklal Street with me, no one said a thing, did a thing. I was invisible then. The solo fat woman traveler in Istanbul is a terrorist. She shocks passersby, and because they can't cry, they laugh.

Marbella 7

Stop re-ly-ing on that bawwww-dy! This is a judge's musically pronounced catchphrase on *RuPaul's Drag Race*, a reality TV show that pits drag queens against each other in weekly challenges. It is a mash-up of *Project Runway* and *America's Next Top Model*, and Ru got to be Tyra, Heidi, and Tim Gunn all at once. Stop re-ly-ing on that bawwww-dy! is what he and his judges will tell contestants who show off their bodies, wearing almost nothing, instead of creating a new look that showcases their fashion aesthetic. If a queen relied on her body, and its own aesthetics, she was in danger of being kicked out, of sashaying away.

The first time I was turned on by drag was when I was an eleven-year-old, visiting Spain with my family. On the beach, I thought the topless women were men, because I didn't understand that women could go topless, too. At the hotel room, Madonna's "Express Yourself" video came on every hour, and I ached at the sight of her in a suit and white socks. The year before, I'd watched the video for "Borderline" and twirled round and round in my room. I loved Madonna's body: her fluorescent shoes, her tummy, her jangling arms jerking off a spray-paint bottle. I twirled round and round, my dress flying up and showing off my panties. I loved doing this. A neighbor boy watched me. Later, he asked me why I liked copying American pop stars. I told him I wasn't. He said, Then how do you explain showing off your underwear shamelessly?

Much, much later, a man in the audience of a talk I was giving with three other Arab women asked us, But isn't feminism, this reclamation of our bodies—isn't all that Western? My friend G responded, Sir, it's not Western to want to be treated equally and to want full rights over our bodies.

Istanbul 8
Before I visited Istanbul, I thought cartoon images of the Orient, where skylines sparkled with domes and minarets, were

Orientalist and inaccurate. That changed when our airport bus turned a sharp corner and I was confronted with just such a skyline, complete with seagulls and sunset and the glitter of the Bosphorus. My first night, I walked to the water and ate dinner at a seafood bar. In order to arrive there, I passed a cluster of silver anchors, fish heads, stray cats that were mostly orange tabbies, and a fish market. Unlike in Cairo, I was able to sit alone, a woman, and nobody bothered me. I ordered a beer. I drank the beer. I smoked cigarettes. Across the water I saw the Hagia Sophia and a few days later, I was inside. The mosque's interior was cool and bright. On the walls were murals of the Virgin Mary and of Jesus. The chandeliers that hung down were geometrically placed in grids and the order was beautiful. The mosque also had a resident cat.

Walking there or to the spice market, men openly stared, assessing my body. It felt as if they were feasting on it. I was uncomfortable with this, since it hadn't happened at the seafood bar. But from that point on, whenever I traveled alone, men stared.

The stray dogs of Istanbul were tagged. Each had a plastic yellow tag pierced into its left ear.

In Istanbul I met L, an electronic music artist, twice. The first time was when he was dressed in linen trousers and a shirt, his head clean-shaven and his feet in sandals. We were on a ferry, and he told me about his work. We were traveling from the European side to the Asian side. We ate stuffed squash flowers and fragrant rice.

A week later we met again, at the building where I was doing my residency. I had been writing about drag, and the women who ran the residency decided to tell everyone to arrive in drag. Everyone did, or at least arrived ready to be put in makeup, except L. L arrived in a gold dress, legs smooth, gold shoes, a black wig, and makeup. His nails were red and long. His chest was padded. I fed him ice cream while he sat in my lap. He came up to my bedroom with me and we stood in the dark, him expecting me to be dominant, me knowing I could have him and being too afraid to bridge the small physical distance between us. We spent the night with friends on the balcony, and I rubbed his beautiful legs and stroked the arch of his foot in the heels.

23

LOVE IS X COUNTRY

In mid-July 2016, I was drinking tea at an Arab- and queer-owned coffee shop called The Bottom Line in Detroit. I drove here straight from St. Louis, through a thunderstorm. Later, K will take me to a jazz club and D will meet us there and tell us stories about her mother. We will stop at a gas station for cigarettes and the Arab guy will look at all three of us and say, Lebanese, Chaldean, Palestinian, pointing at K, D, and me. K won't be impressed; she'll say later that we should've gone to the Hot Arab Guy Gas Station two miles away. Detroit was full of white people. Where did they come from? They've bought houses and turned them into Airbnbs. The old train station has windows on it now. Glass, real windows.

The neighbors on the left and the right of K's house had American flags up. The neighbor on the left, walking her dog, stopped to tell me that she was voting for Trump but that she knew Muslims weren't bad people. "Look at your family," she said, pointing at K's house, and I didn't correct her, because I consider K family. "You guys are just like everyone else. Hardworking and kind."

I didn't want to talk to her at all, so I said, "Please don't act welcoming. This is my country."

•

Hillary was officially nominated by the DNC. Everyone that spoke ahead of her in the days leading up to her nomination, especially the people of color—the Khans, Astrid Silva, etc.—were so much more interesting than her. Why, I kept thinking, why would our next president be someone who was married to an ex-president? The ways power in our country remained in a fixed place angered me.

•

The morning after the last day of the convention, I remembered again the day my father chased me around the house with a knife. The neighbors didn't call the police that day. I had to call them myself.

Why do you remember these old things? my mother has said whenever I've reminded her of them, annoyed. There were so many other, happier memories in this house.

I can't help but laugh. My mother, the empath.

•

Later, when Trump won, I imagined, in a terrifying fever dream, my parents' neighbors watching as fascist police dragged my father's Parkinson's-addled body out of his house, our house. I imagined my son and me back in the basement, where we used to live when he was a baby. This time, he was an adult, and I had to make believe, for the sake of the police, that he was my servant to keep him alive.

•

I had almost crossed the entire country, and I felt nowhere near home.

24

ELECTION DAZE

Ann Arbor, Michigan, is where I was in 2008 when Obama won the election, and it was also where I was in 2016 when Trump won the election. While the town had put out fireworks and parties in 2008, this year, Ann Arbor was eerily quiet, the kind of quiet that every parent knows means something terrible and dangerous is happening. In 2008, I was living with a man who would become my husband. In 2016, I was divorced and dating four people.

Two days after Trump won, I drove from Detroit to Toronto to do an event at a bookstore. Before leaving town, I stopped at a food co-op to pick up some nuts and water. In the aisles were white people in performance fleece and hiking boots, losing their shit entirely. "He's going to roll back everything the Democrats did," one said, panicking. Near the soup aisle, a woman cried, and another woman held her, as they both talked about gay marriage bans. It was happening. The angry layer was finally surfacing in America. I had waited for it in 2001 when we invaded Afghanistan, and waited for it in 2003 when we were invading and bombing Iraq for no reason. I used to sit in cafés in Austin, Texas, before my son got out of school, and watch everyone around me living their lives as usual, and I'd wonder why they weren't crying when we were actively killing people, including ourselves, in two meaningless wars.

Now everyone was angry. Everyone was mourning.

The bridge to Canada was easier to cross than the George Washington in New York. I paid a quick toll and showed my passport and was on my way to Toronto. When I arrived, I parked in front of my friend M's apartment. M, a Palestinian Canadian lesbian, hosted me while I was in town. Her door had two funny homemade leftover Halloween decals: one said Halal and the other said Haram. She set up a hookah for me and ordered sushi and we ate and talked about Trump, and M, a lawyer, said, "Well, now leftist white people can save us. Isn't that what they've always wanted?" We laughed and drank tea and talked about our mothers.

In the morning, I met up with my friend F, a Muslim queer woman I'd befriended years before. She'd asked me what I wanted to do, and all I wanted to do was go to a spa and be naked, so that's what we did. We submerged our bodies in the salt water and cried and talked about ways to survive under Trump. She was a Canadian but still worried. She said we would need provisions for internment camps since Trump would want to instate a Muslim ban. For the camps, we said we would start hoarding water, fabrics, spices, and books. That night, I read in a bookstore run by a brown woman; the audience was full of immigrants and queers and immigrant queers. We held each other in that space and afterward went out for Cuban food, which I'd noticed was being cooked by white teenagers. F and M laughed and told me that there were very few Latinx in Canada. After the meal, we asked our waitress to take a photo of us, but while she did, a white guy at the restaurant counter took a photo of us, too. A woman in hijab told me she had noticed him doing it. So I approached him and asked to see his phone. Terrified of me, he handed it over, and I went through his photos. There were four pictures of us. I deleted them, then deleted them from the deleted folder. I told him to wake up and realize that we weren't an exotic exhibit for him to record, that he needed to ask permission before doing anything like this. I wanted to smash his phone but handed it back to him, and he remained unapologetic and performed a confused look until we all left the restaurant.

I didn't want to go back to America in the morning. I drove anyway, and when I arrived at the border, the patrol officer was an Arab American man named Jallad. That was odd, because it was the last name of my childhood friend, but also because it translated to "he who holds the whip." It was too on the nose. He was strict, and he asked me to pop my trunk. He wanted to know what I wrote about. He wanted to know why I had Lebanese stamps in my passport. He did not say, "Welcome home!" When he was through, he waved me into the country, and I drove to the Detroit airport, the entire way thinking about how I belonged to a country that employed a person of my own ethnic background to police me. We were policing *ourselves*. And Trump wasn't even president yet.

Months later, at his inauguration, he will use words no president has ever used. I will take them and make a poem out of them.

Mere hours after I shared the poem, my father texted me. He was proud of the poem. This was the first time he'd been proud of something I published. It took me twenty-three years of writing to make my father proud. And all I needed to do was rework a narcissist's words.

25

HOME

2016: I made it clear across the nation and was now in Connecticut, visiting my parents for two weeks before heading back. My parents, who thought they'd be safe and sound if they moved to a place like Connecticut. My parents, who do not pass for white.

When I arrived my mother opened our home's wooden door and stood there for almost half a minute trying to figure out who I was. She said later she was confused because my face resembled my face as a baby, but with makeup on. When she finally understood that it was me, she laughed and sobbed. It was the first nice surprise I'd ever given my parents at that house. All my surprises there had been awful—me sneaking out of the house, me being pregnant and eighteen, me, two years later, announcing I was moving to Texas with my baby.

My dad stood in the hallway, his face beet red, giggling at my surprise. I hugged him, and he kept repeating, "I miss you. I love you so much."

Sometimes, in my escape from being a mother, I became a daughter, fully. The feeling resembled that of moving house. Instead of inhabiting a home where I was in charge of another person, I inhabited a home where I was the one cared for. At least, that's the wish, the desire. As my parents aged, I recognized that these homes would begin to fit into one another. I would have to mother them while being their daughter. But maybe there was time. Maybe I could still be a child, for a short while longer.

•

And so I got stoned a few days later and we all went for a walk, my parents, my sister, my brother, his wife, and their dog. I love being stoned around my mom because she is naturally high—she notices small things like butterflies, flowers, birds, earrings, clouds, plants, smells, cupcakes. She is the most fun person to be stoned around. We looked at vintage things and then crossed the street and I fell, miscalculating the space between the street and the curb and my foot. I fell forward and landed on my knees, and my hands broke the fall but my head bounced against the sidewalk a little. I was wearing a giant fake flower hairpin, and it absorbed my fall—femme power!—but while I was down there, I saw my dad's shoes and my mom's shoes and my brother's shoes as they rushed over to help me. I was completely fine, and I reassured them that I was all good, but they doted on me. My dad decided to walk to the drugstore across the street to get me some things to clean up my bleeding knee. When he got back, he told me to put my foot up on a park bench, and he slowly took out the alcohol pads and wiped my wound. His hands shook while he tried to open the Band-Aid wrapper. I wanted to take it from him and just do everything myself, but in that moment, I understood that he wanted to care for me, and that I had to let him. So I waited as he slowly opened the Band-Aid wrapper and negotiated the small plastic tabs on the adhesive side. That part took a minute or two. Then he finally stuck the Band-Aid on my knee. And there I was, my foot on that park bench, my wound cleaned and dressed, forty years old and thirty-nine years old and thirty-eight years old and thirty-seven years old and thirty-six years old and thirty-five years old and twenty-nine years old and twenty-six years old and sixteen years old and twelve years old and nine years old and five years old and four years old and three years old and a baby, all healed. Completely loved.

ACKNOWLEDGMENTS

Earlier versions of some of these chapters were published in different forms:

"Bad Muslim," in *BuzzFeed: Reader*

"Biblioclast," in *The Sun*

"Boaters," in *The Rumpus*

"Imagining Myself in Palestine," in *Guernica*

"Inside the Yellow Line," in *The Progressive*

"Loosely Based," in *Utne Reader*

"Love Is X-Country," in *Nasty Women*

"Neither Slave Nor Pharaoh," in *Bitch* magazine

"The Gift," in *Lives: The New York Times Magazine*

"What Love Is" and "Taking the Knife," in *GAY Mag*

I am indebted to these editors for their sensitive comments and suggestions: Roxane Gay, Lisa Factora-Borchers, Tomi Obaro, Samhita Mukhopadhyay, Kate Harding, and Carol Ann Fitzgerald. Many thanks to Alexandra Christie and Jin Auh for their belief in this book, and to my brilliant editor at Catapult, Megha Majumdar, for her smart, kind, precise, and excellent notes and edits. Thanks also to the Lannan Foundation and the Montalvo Arts Center for the space, both literal and creative, that they offered during the making of this book. And to all the friends who keep me company during my ongoing journey: I am so lucky to have such a generous chosen family.

Thank you.

© Wajiha Ibrahim

RANDA JARRAR is the author of the novel *A Map of Home* and the collection of stories *Him, Me, Muhammad Ali*. Her work has appeared in *The New York Times Magazine*, *Salon*, *Bitch*, *BuzzFeed*, and elsewhere. She is a recipient of a Creative Capital Award and an American Book Award, as well as awards and fellowships from the Civitella Ranieri Foundation, the Lannan Foundation, Hedgebrook, PEN, and others. A professor of creative writing and a performer, Jarrar lives in Los Angeles.